Without Equal

The Clocks of Abner Jones of Bloomfield, New York

G. Russell Oechsle

National Association of
WATCH & CLOCK
Collectors, Inc.

Copyright © 2022 by G. Russell Oechsle and the
National Association of Watch & Clock Collectors, Inc.

All rights reserved. No part of this book may be reproduced,
stored in a retrieval system, or transmitted in any form by any means
(electronic, mechanical, photocopying, recording, scanning or otherwise)
without the prior written permission of the publisher.

Published By:
National Association of Watch & Clock Collectors, Inc.
Columbia, PA 17512

Design By:
Andrew Sherman Design
Port Crane, NY 13833

ISBN 979-8-9859967-0-8

Library of Congress Control Number: 2022906019

First Printing
Printed in the United States of America

There are two types of modern clock books. The first is a report on original investigations. The second is a selective rewrite of material already available in other modern books. The present notes are confined to the first type. They may be of some small interest to others in showing how an author of a clock book discovers its facts.

– *Penrose R. Hoopes*, Author of Connecticut Clockmakers
of the Eighteenth Century, *1930*

My play was a complete success. The audience was a failure.
– *Ashleigh Brilliant*, Writer (1933-   )
(Please Note! This is intended to whimsically speak to the
self-doubts of the author, not the talents of the reader!)

It has long been an axiom of mine that the little things
are infinitely the most important.

– *Arthur Conan Doyle*, Author

For Janet, Always

PREFACE

As I noted in the preface to *An Empire in Time: Clocks & Clock Makers of Upstate, New York* (produced with my partner Helen Boyce, National Association of Watch & Clock Collectors, 2003), clock making and merchandising activities in upstate New York, if and when mentioned, have historically been considered primarily as an offshoot or derivative of the Connecticut clock industry. While the reputation is deserved in many respects, this foundational belief led most early researchers to dismiss out of hand otherwise interesting and exceptional craftsmen who worked in upstate New York in the 19th century.

In June 1947, Brooks Palmer, an important researcher and author of *A Treasury of American Clocks* (1967), likely one of the books read by nearly every novice American clock collector in the late 20th century, wrote an article in the *NAWCC Bulletin* entitled "An Ideal American Clock Collection." In Palmer's article, the only New York shelf clocks warranting mention were the Timby Solar Clock (two sentences) and Asa Munger's shelf clocks (one sentence).

Fortunately, respect for notable upstate clockmakers has increased over time, and the huge, flamboyant, unique clocks made by Abner Jones at Bloomfield, NY, have emerged as one of the most intriguing to the cognoscenti. Beyond the clocks, however, Jones the man and maker has remained an enigma. *Where did he come from? When did he make his clocks? Where did he make his clocks? What were his production totals?* All questions asked but, to date, not definitively answered. If the evidence presented in this book is to be believed, no one had it quite right.

My goal has been to accumulate all past research; expand upon that in every way necessary; to run out every lead possible and then to provide all new findings with such detail and accuracy as to do this remarkable clockmaker justice. I hope readers will find this effort a significant addition to their understanding of Abner Jones, with many, many questions answered, numerous problems solved and, to be sure, many new questions to ponder.

While an original work, this Abner Jones manuscript is built on a foundation set by a number of important researchers. Not the least of these was the late Evan Edwards, a Rochester, NY, native who was introduced to Abner Jones clocks in the 1970s and who did much early research, culminating in a presentation at the National Association of Watch & Clock Collectors annual Time Symposium (now named after the esteemed researcher Ward Francillon) at Rochester in 1987. Beginning in the 1970s, Edwards compiled an inventory of every Jones shelf clock he could locate, eventually reaching 39 in number, which he shared with the author and others. When Edwards saw and recorded a clock, he left, on the inside surface of the door of the respective case, his ubiquitous "EAE # ___" identification in magic marker. These numbers did not reflect the relative age or production chronology of the particular clock, but simply the next Jones clock he had seen. All of the clocks Edwards recorded, with the exception of two or three that I have been unable to track down, will be presented, plus a significant number of additional clocks that have come to light more recently.

In addition, the research of a number of others has been extremely beneficial, in particular with respect to the Jones family genealogy. At the author's request, genealogist Robert Manke of Rhode Island jumped full scale into the oft-confusing background of Abner Jones, his father Jacob of Pittsfield, NH, his cousin Richard Jones and others associated with clock making activities in New Hampshire and New York. Manke's unpublished manuscript on the topic will be referenced throughout this work. Similar and additional contributions were offered by Patrick Hagan of Pennsylvania and Frank and Helen Boyce of New York. Such is the interest in Abner Jones and his unique clocks that help was offered freely and often. The cooperation of dozens of owners of Abner Jones clocks has been essential. I am indebted to Patti Philippon and Tom Manning of the American Clock & Watch Museum for their willingness to provide access to the photo archive of Abner Jones clocks compiled by Evan Edwards. Lastly, I am indebted to several great researchers and horologists including Chris Bailey, Mary Jane Dapkus and Tom Grimshaw for their willingness to review the manuscript and make suggestions on this work, and to Laura Taylor, Managing Editor, NAWCC for her final editing. These individuals and many others have assisted in making this book possible. Their names, with apologies to anyone I may have missed, appear at the end of the book.

All photos are by the author unless otherwise noted.

CONTENTS

v **PREFACE**

2 **Chapter One:**
Abner Jones at Pittsfield, New Hampshire

7 **Chapter Two:**
Abner Jones and Richard Jones at
East Bloomfield, NY – 1818-1828
A Homestead and Two Marriages; The Bloomfield Homestead; The Location; Early Clock Making at Bloomfield; Tall Clocks 1-4; Abner and Richard Jones – Clock Making in an Era of Change

24 **Chapter Three:**
A New Enterprise - 1828-33
Abner Jones at Bloomfield; Clock Making Resumes; Asa v. Abner; Clues; What Came First?; The Group One Clocks; Conclusions

55 **Chapter Four:**
Shelf Clock Transitions – 1833-35
Group Two Clocks

64 **Chapter Five:**
1835 - Clock Making Begins at
West Bloomfield
Clock Making in Context; The Clocks of 1835

78 **Chapter Six:**
A New Standard
The Group Four Clocks; An Anomaly on Its Face

89 **Chapter Seven:**
Who Made the Shelf Clock Cases?

92 **Chapter Eight:**
Late Cornice Top Cases Without Drawers
Part One: Group Five Clocks; A.C. Totman – The Abner Jones Clock Repairer of Record; Part Two: Group Six Clocks

112 **Chapter Nine:**
Late Cornice Top Cases With Drawers
Part One: The Group Seven Clocks; Part Two: The Group Eight Clocks

126 **Chapter Ten:**
Basics, Anomalies and Speculations
Movement Gear Counts; Movement Back Plate Cutouts; Bracketology; Plate Pillar Posts; Weights; Keys; Door Closures; Drawer Pulls; Door Pulls; Hands; Shelf Clocks by the Numbers

149 **Chapter Eleven:**
Full Empire Clocks and Abner's Opus

160 **Chapter Twelve:**
The Time Ends for Clock Making at Bloomfield

163 **In Conclusion:**
Without Equal: The Clocks of Abner Jones
of Bloomfield, New York

APPENDICES

165 **Appendix A:** Group One Clock Characteristics

166 **Appendix B:** Group Two Clock Characteristics

167 **Appendix C:** Group Three Clock Characteristics

168 **Appendix D:** Group Four Clock Characteristics

169 **Appendix E:** Group Five Clock Characteristics

170 **Appendix F:** Group Six Clock Characteristics

171 **Appendix G:** Group Seven Clock Characteristics

172 **Appendix H:** Group Eight Clock Characteristics

173 **Appendix I:** Evan Edwards' Inventory of
Abner Jones Clocks

175 **Appendix J:** Abner Jones Shelf Clocks
by the Numbers

176 **RESEARCH ILLUSTRATIONS**

178 **ACKNOWLEDGEMENTS**

179 **INDEX**

CHAPTER ONE

Abner Jones at Pittsfield, New Hampshire

Abner Jones was born August 24, 1789, at Pittsfield, NH, the son of Jacob and Hannah (Sealy) Jones. His father, Jacob, was born September 30, 1749, the son of John Jones (1724-1815) and Hannah Dow (1728-1806), both of whom settled in Pittsfield from Seabrook, NH, with fellow Quakers in the late 1700s. Jacob Jones was a brass tall clockmaker, the first at Pittsfield according to historical records. Jacob received his training at the hands of clockmaker Daniel Balch of Bradford and Newburyport, MA.[1] The location of Pittsfield in Merrimack County, NH, is shown in *Figure 1*.[2]

Abner Jones was the youngest of 11 children of Jacob and Hannah, and the sixth son. His brothers included Joseph (1775-1842); Jacob (1776-1850); John (1780-1861); Nathan (1784-1860) and Jonathan (1787-unknown), and his sisters included Mary (1777-1855); Bildad (1780-); Hannah (~1782-); Miriam (~1785-), and Huldah (~1785-1850).[3]

Sources identify several of Jacob's sons as having followed him in clock making, including Joseph, Jonathan and Abner. In addition, Jacob's grandson James by son Jacob was reported to have been involved in the trade.[4] The Jones family tree reflecting the known clockmakers is shown in *Figure 2*.

E. Harold Young's *History of Pittsfield, NH*, (Town of Pittsfield, NH, 1953) states that Jacob Jones established his home and clock manufactory in the Knowlton Corners area of Pittsfield, east of the village and near the Quaker Meeting House. The book features a picture of the Jones home as it stood in forlorn condition at the time the book was being prepared. Young states that *"In the house by the side of the old Lock road, so called, the famous Jacob Jones clocks came into being under the deft fingers of their maker. The fact that Jacob Jones worked here is vouched by the presence of pounds of brass filings under the floor of the front room to the right of the door. These filings were found in later years when the floor was removed for shoring and replacement."*[6]

Despite the bedraggled appearance of the Jones house in Young's *History*, (*see Figure 3*), Pittsfield Town Historian Larry Berkson was able to provide pictures to prove that it is still in existence, if somewhat modified, at Pittsfield (*see Figure 4*).[7]

Figure 1

Map of Merrimack County, NH, with the Town of Pittsfield (in shading).

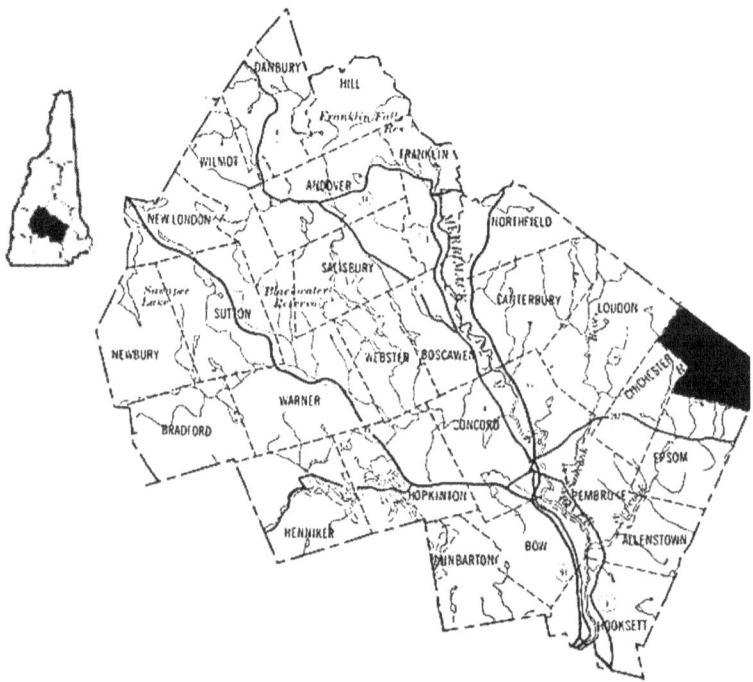

Figure 2

The Abner Jones family tree reflecting the clockmaker descendants of John Jones • Source: Robert Manke[5]

John Jones
B. May 11, 1724, Amesbury, MA
M. Oct. 13, 1748, Amesbury, MA
to Hannah Dow
D. Mar. 28, 1815, Pittsfield, NH

 Jacob Jones
B. Dec. 30, 1749, Kingston, NH
M. Jan. 1, 1774, Pittsfield, NH,
to Hannah Cilley
D. Jul. 25, 1839, Pittsfield, NH

Joseph Jones
B. Mar. 7, 1775, Pittsfield, NH
M. Jan. 13, 1796, Chichester, NH,
to Dolly Hilyard
D. Oct. 31, 1842, Pittsfield, NH

Jacob Jones
B. ~1776, Kingston, NH
M. Dec. 29, 1799, Northwood, NH,
to Nancy Anna Rollins
D. May 1850, Pittsfield, NH

Jonathan Jones
B. Oct. 16, 1787, Gilford, NH
M(1). Jan. 31, 1809, Andover, NH,
to Elizabeth Brown
D. Unknown

Abner Jones
B. Aug. 24, 1789, Pittsfield, NH
M. Oct. 16, 1820, Bloomfield, NY,
to Sabra Hickox
D. Aug. 24, 1876, Avon, NY

Richard Jones
B. May 2, 1796, Chichester, NH
M. ~1820
to Lucy Ann Hickox
D. 1846, Livingston City, NY

James Jones
B. Nov. 29, 1810, Pittsfield, NH
M. ~1832
to Hannah Louise Marston
D. Aug. 5, 1885, Pittsfield, NH

 Reported in the clock trade

The Two Abners

Ascertaining facts from historical records is perhaps difficult enough without compounding factors such as your subject being confused with another individual with the same name, who is nearly the same age, is engaged in the same trade, and who lives in the same geographical area.

All of those factors are in play here, as our Abner Jones has in nearly all previous research efforts been confused with another Abner who was a third cousin. This "other" Abner Jones was 3 years younger, was also a verified clockmaker and lived and operated in Weare, NH, located approximately 30 miles southwest of Pittsfield in northern Hillsborough County, New Hampshire.

Clock historian Chris Bailey was perhaps the first to definitively state that there were, indeed, two distinct Abner Jones clockmakers in his important work *Two Hundred Years of American Clocks and Watches*, in 1975.[8] Individual research by Evan Edwards,[9] verified most recently by Robert Manke,[10] has clearly identified the relationship. Our Abner Jones of Pittsfield shared a great-grandfather, John Jones (1684-1711) of Amesbury, MA, with the other Abner Jones of Weare, NH. John Jones had two sons – John, grandfather of our Abner, and Abner, grandfather of the Abner of Weare, making them third cousins. The relationship is shown in ***Figure 5***.

A further distinction between Abner of Pittsfield and Abner of Weare can be seen through a comparison of their clock movements. Our Abner's clocks understandably resemble those produced by his father, Jacob, while those made by Abner of Weare bear little resemblance to either maker.

Figure 3
Jacob Jones homestead, Pittsfield, NH, ca. 1950

Photo Courtesy Town of Pittsfield, NH: Young's History of Pittsfield, NH, 1953

Figure 4
The Jones family homestead ca. 2020

Photo Courtesy Larry Berkson, Pittsfield, NH, Town Historian

Figure 5
Jones family tree showing the two branches of clockmakers • Source: Robert Manke

John Jones
B. Feb. 24, 1684, Amesbury, MA
M. May. 29, 1711, Amesbury, MA to Susanna Fowler
D. 1750, Amesbury, MA

John Jones
B. May 11, 1724, Amesbury, MA
M. Oct. 13, 1748, Amesbury, MA to Hannah Dow
D. Mar. 28, 1815, Pittsfield, NH

Abner Jones
B. June 4, 1774, Amesbury, MA
M. Jan. 11, 1749, Salem, MA to Abigail Buxton
D. Dec. 21, 1814, Amesbury, MA

 Jacob Jones
B. Dec. 30, 1749, Kingston, NH
M. Jan. 1, 1774, Pittsfield, NH, to Hannah Cilley
D. Jul. 25, 1839, Pittsfield, NH

Capt. John Jones
B. Apr. 27, 1753, Kingston, NH
M. Between 1800-1810 to Mehitabel Barton
D. Unknown

Joseph Jones
B. Jul. 9, 1761, Amesbury, MA
M. Oct. 3, 1781, to Ruth Gove
D. Unknown

Joseph Jones
B. Mar. 7, 1775, Pittsfield, NH
M. Jan. 13, 1796, Chichester, NH, to Dolly Hilyard
D. Oct. 31, 1842, Pittsfield, NH

Jacob Jones
B. ~1776, Kingston, NH
M. Dec. 29, 1799, Northwood, NH, to Nancy Anna Rollins
D. May 1850, Pittsfield, NH

Jonathan Jones
B. Oct. 16, 1787, Gilford, NH
M(1). Jan. 31, 1809, Andover, NH, to Elizabeth Brown
D. Unknown

Abner Jones
B. Aug. 24, 1789, Pittsfield, NH
M. Oct. 16, 1820, Bloomfield, NY, to Sabra Hickox
D. Aug. 24, 1876, Avon, NY

Abner Jones
B. Jul. 14, 1792, Weare, NH
M. Aug. 3, 1815, Weare, NH, to Phebe Breed
D. Apr. 22, 1853, Lynn, MA

Richard Jones
B. May 2, 1796, Chichester, NH
M. ~1820 to Lucy Ann Hickox
D. 1846, Livingston City, NY

James Jones
B. Nov. 29, 1810, Pittsfield, NH
M. ~1832 to Hannah Louise Marston
D. Aug. 5, 1885, Pittsfield, NH

 Reported in the clock trade

A fine tall clock by Jacob Jones is shown in **Figures 6-8**, which depict, clockwise from left, *a close-up of the bonnet and dial, the beautiful mahogany and maple tall clock case, and the 8-day brass movement*.

Compare the Jacob Jones 8-day brass tall clock movement shown here with one produced by his son Abner at Bloomfield, NY (**Figure 9**) and an example by Abner Jones of Weare, NH (**Figure 10**). There are clear similarities between the clocks by father and son, including the unusual use of brass for all of the strike levers, and obvious differences between both of those clocks and the construction of the Weare-produced clock.

Figures 6 – 8
A Jacob Jones, Pittsfield, NH, tall clock.

Photos courtesy Delaney's Antique Clocks

Figure 9
Abner Jones (NY) tall clock movement

Figure 10
Abner Jones (Weare, NH) movement

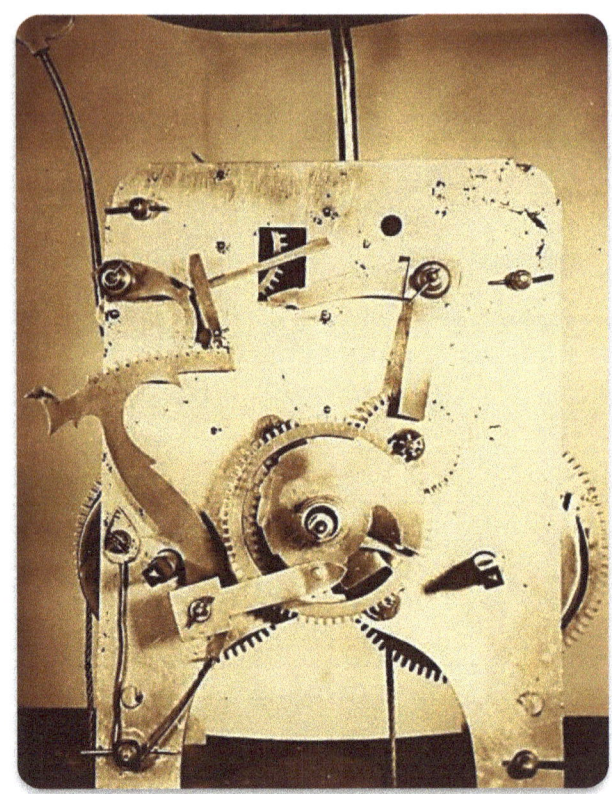

Photo courtesy Charles Parsons.
New Hampshire Clocks & Clockmakers,
Adams Brown Co. Exeter, NH, 1976

---

[1] Manke, Robert. *Genealogy of Abner Jones of Pittsfield*, (unpublished manuscript, November 2018), from a biography of Jacob Jones authored by Sharon Rodgers on Ancestry.com.

[2] Map Source: US Soil Conservation Service, 1980. Library of Congress Geography & Map Division, On Line Catalog.

[3] Ibid. Taken from *NH Birth Index* and Family Trees on Ancestry.com.

[4] Parsons, Charles S. *New Hampshire Clocks & Clockmakers*, Adams Brown Co., Exeter, NH, 1976

[5] Manke. Manke's source for the clockmaker attributions come from Parsons and from the biography of Jacob Jones by Sharon Rodgers noted previously.

[6] Young, E. Harold. *History of Pittsfield, New Hampshire*, 1953, Town of Pittsfield & Harold Young.

[7] Personal Correspondence with Larry Berkson.

[8] Bailey, Chris. *Two Hundred Years of American Clocks and Watches*, A Rutledge Book, Prentice-Hall, Inc. 1975, p. 82.

[9] Edwards, Evan. *Abner Jones Clockmaker* (unpublished manuscript, August, 1982).

[10] Manke. Taken from Chichester, NH, Vital Records; Census Records for NY, and *FindAGrave.com*.

CHAPTER TWO

Abner Jones and Richard Jones at Bloomfield, NY – 1818-1828

J.H. French's *Gazetteer of the State of New York* (1860) notes that Bloomfield was one of the early towns of Ontario County, NY; sections were taken off to form the new towns of Victor and Mendon (1812) and then what remained was further subdivided into the current towns of East and West Bloomfield in 1833. The *Gazetteer* described Bloomfield as *"an interior town, lying n.w. of the center of [Ontario County]. Its surface is rolling, with a gentle inclination toward the n. The ridges are 50 to 600 feet above the valleys…The soil is a deep, fertile, gravelly loam…."*[1] **Figures 11 and 12** show the location of Ontario County in New York State, and the current towns of East and West Bloomfield in Ontario County, respectively.

Figures 11 & 12

Maps showing Ontario County in New York State and East and West Bloomfield in Ontario County, respectively.

Source: *Wikipedia*

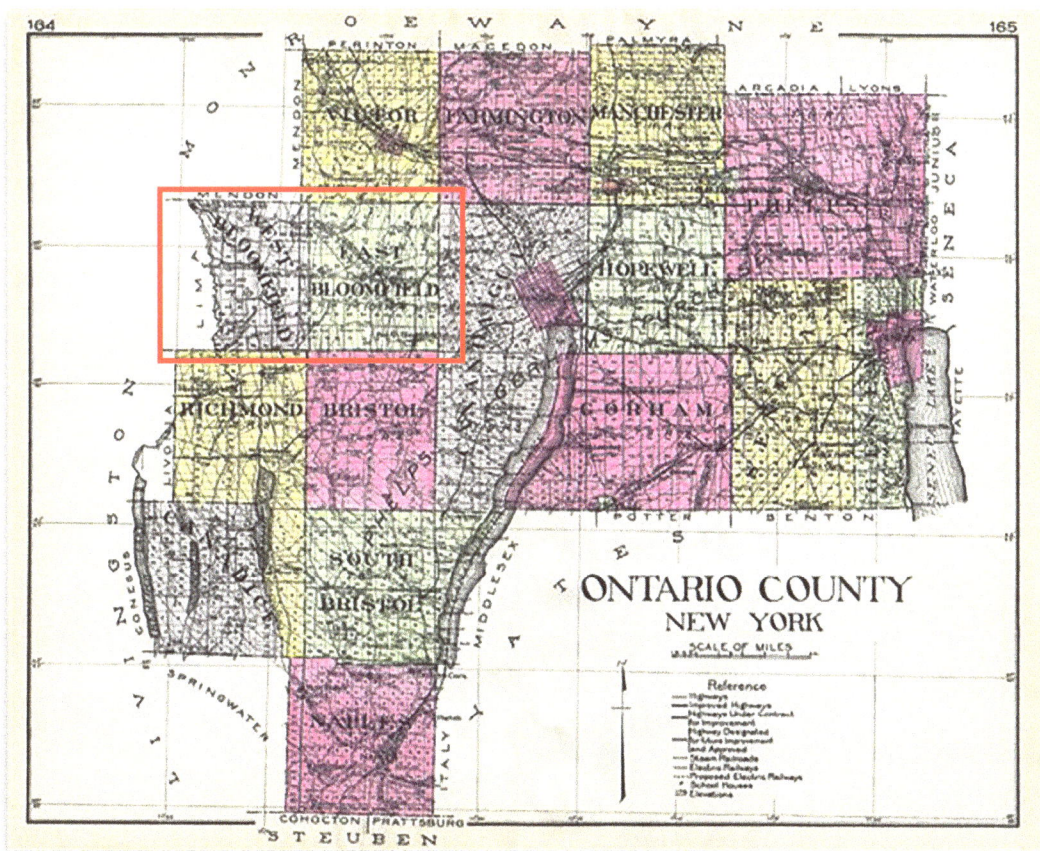

Source: *New Century Atlas of the Counties of the State of New York* (Century Map Company, Philadelphia, PA, 1912.)
Library of Congress Map Collection

Chapter Two • 7

East Bloomfield was an established village by 1820, with churches, artisans and manufactories largely owing to the surrounding rich agricultural resources and its favorable location on the Ontario and Genesee Turnpike.[2] This major road was established in 1805 and ran from Canandaigua, the Ontario County seat located just east of Bloomfield, west to Buffalo. The Seneca Turnpike and other improved roads ran east from Canandaigua through Central New York to Albany.[3] This was the likely route taken by Abner Jones to Bloomfield. The original turnpike route through Bloomfield is today jointly followed by major roads NY Route 5 and U.S. Route 20.

Evidence supports the fact that Abner Jones relocated from Pittsfield, NH, to Bloomfield, NY, in 1818, when he would have been 29 years of age. Pittsfield tax records support the 1818 date. All of the adult males, including Abner, in the Jacob Jones family were taxed at Pittsfield in 1817, but no listing for Abner appears in 1818 or thereafter.[4]

Apparently accompanying Abner in his move west was *Richard* Jones, an individual essentially unidentified until recent work by genealogist Robert Manke. His research has proven that Richard was Abner's nephew, the son of Abner's brother Joseph.[5] Their relationship is shown in *Figure 13*. As his brother Joseph was fully 14 years older than Abner, Joseph's son Richard, born in 1796, was only 7 years younger than Abner, so by age they were more akin to brothers.

The most definitive record of the arrival of Abner and, in all likelihood, Richard in 1818 was an advertisement appearing over the course of several months in mid to late 1818 in *The Ontario Repository*, published by James D. Bemis at Canandaigua.[6] The ad reads as follows, with the actual copy shown in *Figure 14*.

Brass Foundery, &c.
THE subscribers have established a BRASS FOUNDERY, in the brick building, near the meeting-house, in East Bloomfield; where they will manufacture Shovels and Tongs, Andirons, Fenders, Clock Work, Sleigh Bells, and other brass Castings.

They also make or repair CLOCKS and WATCHES, in a faithful manner.

They purchase old Copper, Brass, Pewter and Blocktin, at a fair price.

PAGE & JONES. 3m15
Bloomfield, July 18, 1818.

According to the Town of East Bloomfield Historian Judi Stewart, the "Meeting House" referred to was a church building just north of the East Bloomfield Congregational Church, which is located at the intersection of today's Routes 20 and 5 and South Avenue in the village of East Bloomfield. The Meeting House was removed in 1838

Figure 13

Jones family tree showing the relationship between Abner and Richard Jones • Source: Robert Manke

John Jones
B. May 11, 1724, Amesbury, MA
M. Oct. 13, 1748, Amesbury, MA to Hannah Dow
D. Mar. 28, 1815, Pittsfield, NH

Jacob Jones
B. Dec. 30, 1749, Kingston, NH
M. Jan. 1, 1774, Pittsfield, NH, to Hannah Cilley
D. Jul. 25, 1839, Pittsfield, NH

Joseph Jones
B. Mar. 7, 1775, Pittsfield, NH
M. Jan. 13, 1796, Chichester, NH, to Dolly Hilyard
D. Oct. 31, 1842, Pittsfield, NH

Jacob Jones
B. ~1776, Kingston, NH
M. Dec. 29, 1799, Northwood, NH, to Nancy Anna Rollins
D. May 1850, Pittsfield, NH

Jonathan Jones
B. Oct. 16, 1787, Gilford, NH
M(1). Jan. 31, 1809, Andover, NH, to Elizabeth Brown
D. Unknown

Abner Jones
B. Aug. 24, 1789, Pittsfield, NH
M. Oct. 16, 1820, Bloomfield, NY, to Sabra Hickox
D. Aug. 24, 1876, Avon, NY

Richard Jones
B. May 2, 1796, Chichester, NH
M. ~1820 to Lucy Ann Hickox
D. 1846, Livingston City, NY

James Jones
B. Nov. 29, 1810, Pittsfield, NH
M. ~1832 to Hannah Louise Marston
D. Aug. 5, 1885, Pittsfield, NH

 Reported in the clock trade

Figure 14

Advertisement for the partnership of Page & Jones at the village of East Bloomfield dated July, 1818 as it appeared in The Ontario Repository *published at Canadaigua, NY.*

> **Brass Foundery, &c.**
>
> THE subscribers have established a BRASS FOUNDERY, in the brick building, near the meeting-house, in East-Bloomfield, where they will manufacture Shovels and Tongs, Andirons, Fenders, Clock Work, Sleigh Bells, and other brass Castings.
>
> They also make or repair CLOCKS and WATCHES, in a faithful manner.
>
> ☞ They purchase old Copper, Brass, Pewter and Block tin, at a fair price.
>
> PAGE & JONES.
>
> Bloomfield, July 18, 1818.   3m15

for the construction of the three-story brick and stone Bloomfield Academy, which today is the home of the East Bloomfield Historical Society.[7] The brick building where the Jones foundry was located was reportedly torn down in 1835.[8] A residence is on the site today. *Figure 15* shows the East Bloomfield Green, Congregational Church, Academy and the presumed original location of the brick foundry building location (shown as the house lot of R. C. Munson) as of 1859.[9]

The Mr. "Page" referred to in the ad is as yet a complete unknown. Several individuals appear in the Bloomfield records with that surname, but no definite ties to Abner or Richard Jones have been identified to date.

One possible candidate is **Leonard Page**, who is the only individual with that surname listed in the *1820 Census for the Town of Bloomfield*. The *Census* records Page as being involved in "manufacturing."[10]

Leonard Page is not listed in either the 1810 or 1830 Census for Bloomfield. Quelling enthusiasm to a significant degree is the fact that extant records show that he was a resident of West Bloomfield, not East Bloomfield. Only two deed transactions appear in the records for Leonard. In November, 1812, he purchased a small house lot on the road leading north from the West Bloomfield village center for $27.50 from owner Leon Wait.[11] He sold that lot to Allen Willey in March, 1816 for $40.[12] Leonard Page was still living at West Bloomfield in 1820; he was recorded in the midst of other West Bloomfield village residents in the 1820 *Census*. No other records for this Mr. Page have been uncovered by the author. A check of any possible New Hampshire ties between the Joneses and Mr. Page has also proven fruitless.

Yet another Mr. Page warrants some mention and perhaps appears more relevant. This individual, **Stephen Page**, clearly operated in the village of East Bloomfield and had tantalizing ties to a number of individuals associated with Abner Jones, if not with Jones himself. Unfortunately, his name does not appear in the 1810 or 1820 *Census* records for Bloomfield, and while he may have been absent when the enumerator showed up in 1820, this nonetheless creates cause for doubt.[13]

Figure 15

The village green of East Bloomfield as of 1859. To the west of the village green (labeled "Park") is, looking south to north, the Congregational Church, East Bloomfield Academy, and the house lot of R.C. Munson, former location of the "brick building" in which the Joneses operated their foundry.

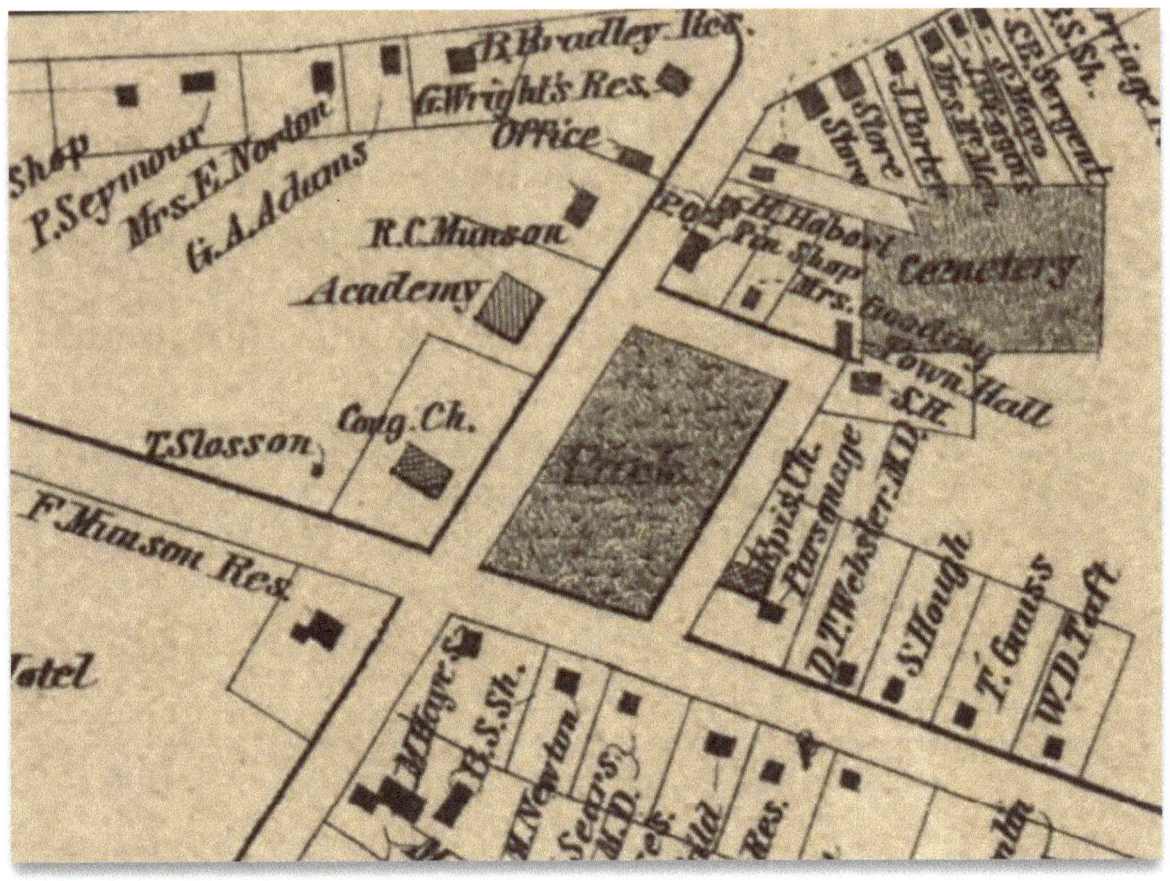

Unlike Leonard Page, Stephen was a party to a detailed list of property transactions at East Bloomfield, the earliest of which dates to April, 1823, when he purchased a one acre house lot in Lot #38 in the village from Daniel Miles for $100.[14] Intriguingly, this house lot shared a property line with the residence at that time of *Abner and Richard Jones*, and the seller, Mr. Miles, has been identified anecdotally as having been a casemaker for a circa 1820 Abner Jones tall clock (see further discussion on both points later in this chapter).

Page sold this lot in September, 1826 to Mary Turner for $200, and one year later he purchased two lots on the East Bloomfield Village Green containing a house and a commercial building from Harvey Hobert for $300. These lots were just a corner of the Green away from the Meeting House and the apparent Jones foundry site. The facts combine to create images of potential ties to Abner Jones until it is realized that Page owned these lots for only two months, selling both to Harlow Munson on December 26, 1827, for $310, pocketing a $10 profit.[15]

Stephen Page does appear in the *1830 Census for Bloomfield*, listed as being between the ages of 40 and 49.[16] Deed records show that he purchased multiple farm parcels in the town in 1831 and 1832 totaling over 200 acres. He sold all of his land holdings in April, 1835 to Henry Munson for the substantial sum of $5,500, and one month later purchased a house lot in East Bloomfield from Henry Mandeville for $200.[17] In April, 1837, Stephen advertised that he had been deserted by his wife, Emma, leaving him with three young children.[18] Stephen died on October 12, 1839. Probate papers filed by Stephen's daughter Sarah, upon coming of age, indicate he was intestate and with "poor chattel and credits." His children were put into the guardianship of Chauncey W. Markham and Josiah Porter.[19]

As such, the identity of Mr. Page remains unclear.

A Homestead and Two Marriages

The *1820 U.S. Census for the Town of Bloomfield* almost records the names of both Abner and Richard Jones. A review of the census document page for the town of Bloomfield (*see Figure 16*) actually only notes the name of *Richard* as the nominal head of household, (Line 375) but does record in that household two adult males, one between the ages of 16 and 25 (this would fit with Richard) and one between 26 and 40 (this would fit with Abner). Also noted were two females between the ages of 16 and 25.[20]

The *Census* records the two males as being involved in "manufacturing." As for the two females, this appears to be the first listing of Richard and Abner's wives Lucy and Sabra, respectively.

Edwards reports that Richard Jones and Lucy Hickox of Bloomfield were married in May, 1820, and that Abner married Lucy's sister Sabra on October 16, 1820, both ceremonies taking place in the Bloomfield Congregational Church.[21] According to later *Census* records, Lucy was born in late 1803, so of the "two females between the age of 16 and 25" in 1820, she would have been 16. Based on that fact and lacking any other primary source information, her sister Sabra would have been the older of the two. A later reference records their father's name as William Hickox, a farmer in West Bloomfield.[22]

In addition to the *1820 Census*, several property transactions that year document Abner and Richard's residency at Bloomfield. These transactions were not, however, for their primary residence, but for an adjacent one acre lot. The first deed, dated March 25, 1820, states that "*John Adams of Bloomfield… the party of the first part* [sold to] *Abner Jones and Richard Jones of the same place, parties of the second part*" one acre of land **adjacent** to a lot "*formerly owned by Peter Brown* [actually Bowen] *but now the lands of the parties of the second part*" (i.e. the property already occupied by Abner and Richard) in Lot #38 in Bloomfield for $300.[23]

The *1810 Census* records Peter Bowen as living next to resident Abner Adams in the settled area of the village of East Bloomfield.[24] Abner Adams' property was located in Lot #39 of the Phelps and Gorham's Purchase and the Peter Bowen lot straddled the east edge of Lot #39 and west edge of Lot #38 (*see Figure 17* for more clarification).

It appears that no deed was recorded when Abner and Richard settled at Bloomfield on or around 1818. While it was not uncommon for many late 18th and early 19th century property transactions to go unrecorded, in this instance that possibility was relatively small, as Ontario County had a law in effect, first passed in 1798, years before most other counties in upstate New York, which required all deeds to be recorded.[25] So if no deed was recorded, one other option exists, and that is the possibility, if not likelihood, that Abner and Richard rented or leased their homestead from Abner Adams. This appears to be the case, as Abner Adams purchased what was to become the Abner and Richard Jones homestead from Peter Bowen in 1817[26] and is recorded as having eventually sold it to Austin Avery on May 17, 1824.[27] The evidence, therefore, supports the likelihood that Abner and Richard Jones lived at this rented or leased homestead from 1818 to early 1824.

Abner and Richard held onto the one acre lot purchased from John Adams for only seven months, selling it on October 30, 1820 (at an apparent loss) for $200 to Bloomfield resident Daniel W. Buel. As shown in *Figure 16*, Buel is noted as a neighbor in the *1820 Census*.

Figure 16

Page from the 1820 U.S. Census for Bloomfield, NY, showing the listing for Richard Jones and others.

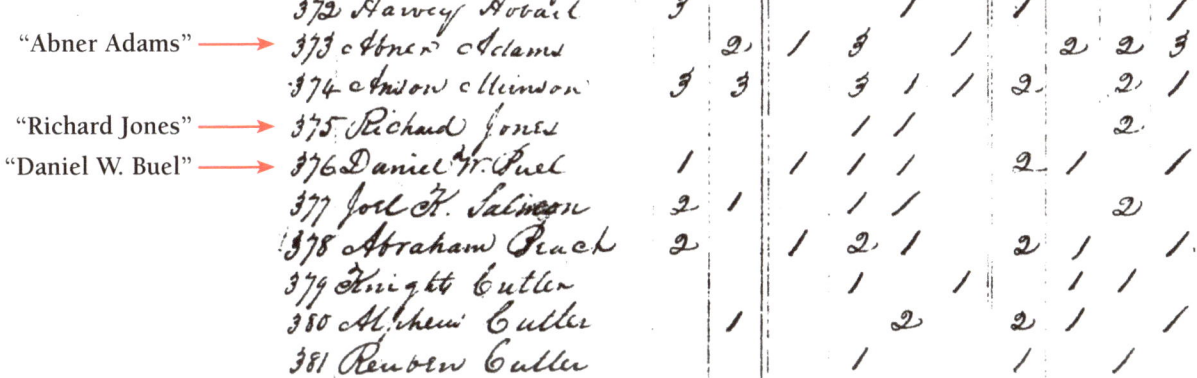

This second deed lists the parties of the first part (the sellers) as "Abner Jones *and Sabra his wife* and Richard Jones *and Lucy his wife* [emphasis added] of Bloomfield in the County of Ontario."[28] Thus the recorded dates for the marriages of Richard and Lucy (May, 1820) and Abner and Sabra (October 16, 1820) conform with the language of the lot purchase of March 25, 1820, when no wives were mentioned, and the sale date of October, 30, 1820, when both wives were included.

The Location

As noted, the *1820 Census* shows (*see Figure 16*) that Abner Adams was a close neighbor of the Joneses. Based on that proximity, historic Bloomfield maps showing property locations were sought to help identify the exact location of the first Jones homestead at East Bloomfield. Unfortunately, the earliest map found by the author was published in 1852, but the search was helped by the fact that the circa 1820 Abner Adams homestead (owned by "M." – Myron – Adams in 1852) is clearly marked on this and other subsequent maps (*see Figure 17* for the Abner Adams house as it appears today). A partial map of the village of East Bloomfield from the *1852 Map of Ontario County, New York*, published by H. F. Walling of Philadelphia after a survey by John E. Gillett, is shown in **Figure 18**.[29]

The 1852 map shows two residences just northeast of the Adams home. The westerly of those two houses seems likely to have been the first home of Abner and Richard Jones at Bloomfield and that the lot and home just to the east was the early to mid-1820s property of Daniel Buel, then of Daniel Miles and then later of Stephen Page.

With the sale by Abner Adams to Austin Avery of their rented homestead in May, 1824, it can be presumed that Abner, Richard and their families moved to a new property in Bloomfield. The evidence supporting their likely new home will be provided in **Chapter Three**.

The next available Ontario County map was published in 1859 by A.R.Z. Dawson of Philadelphia from a survey by D.G. Beers. A portion of that map covering the same area as **Figure 18** is shown in **Figure 19**.[30]

Considerable changes can be noted in the 1859 map. Most importantly, both of the houses shown to the northeast of the Adams home and just east of the west line of "Lot 38" in 1852 are now missing, perhaps indicating that the homes were removed or otherwise destroyed between 1852 and 1859.

Figure 17

The historic Abner Adams house as it appears today.

Figure 18

1852 Map of Ontario County *showing detail of the Village of East Bloomfield. The location of the previous homestead of Abner Adams (shown as owned by M. [Myron] Adams in 1852), and the likely location of the Jones homestead are indicated.*

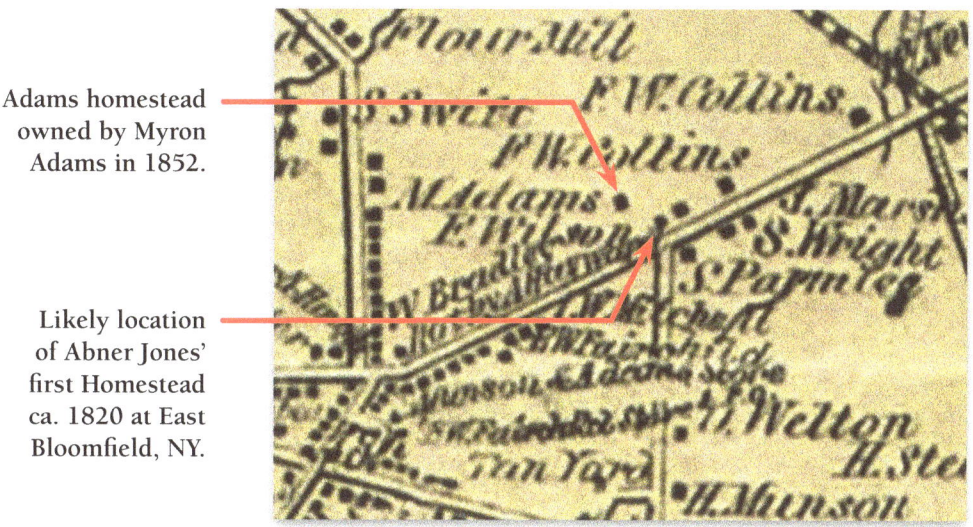

Adams homestead owned by Myron Adams in 1852.

Likely location of Abner Jones' first Homestead ca. 1820 at East Bloomfield, NY.

Figure 19

Portion of the 1859 Map of Ontario County *showing the same area of the Village of Bloomfield shown in Figure 18 with notable property changes.*

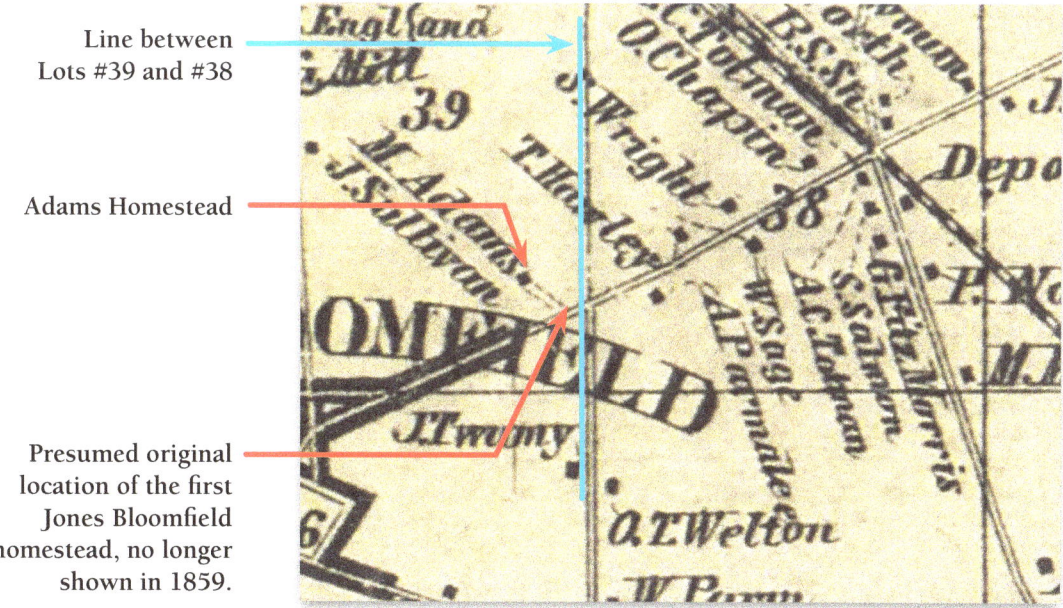

Line between Lots #39 and #38

Adams Homestead

Presumed original location of the first Jones Bloomfield homestead, no longer shown in 1859.

Early Clock Making at Bloomfield

Based on the evidence at hand, it can now be clearly assumed that both Abner and Richard Jones were trained brass founders and clockmakers when they arrived at Bloomfield, NY, and that they engaged in "manufacturing" upon their arrival. What will remain open to speculation is why they left New Hampshire; why, when they did so, did they choose this particular frontier area of upstate New York as their new home, and, lastly, who, again, was the early partner Mr. Page?

As for Abner and Richard, with a half dozen or so close relatives in the trade in New Hampshire, a move west clearly offered the prospect of less competition. As for why Bloomfield, we will likely never know. The *1820 Census for Bloomfield, NY,* does list three other "Jones" living there, including Elias, Charles and Philip, but none of those individuals could be linked to the Pittsfield, NH, family, nor are any New Hampshire links to the elusive Mr. Page evident.[31] Perhaps the pair simply traveled west and stopped when they found an upland location that reminded them of home.

To the residents of a new settlement, the addition of a brass foundry was clearly advantageous. Rather than outsourcing items from afar, a new foundry operation could provide an immediate supply of everyday items such as locks, hinges, gears, bearings, knobs, pulls, horns, etc. and, of course, from the training Abner and Richard had received, they could make clock movements, pulleys, hands, pendulum bobs, keys and weights. Their 1818 advertisement added shovels, tongs, andirons, fenders and sleigh bells to the commodity list.

The clocks made by Abner and Richard Jones were 8-day brass tall (aka "grandfather") clock movements with accessories which were then housed in individually built wooden cases generally procured from local cabinet makers. As a result, no two tall clock cases with Jones' New York movements found to date are identical. Unlike Jacob Jones, Abner and Richard chose not to inscribe their names on their clock dials; nor do their dial sources provide any consistent style from which to give a clue as to the movement maker. The only way to clearly distinguish their product from any other contemporary maker is to examine the clock movement itself, not a simple task. As we will see, however, unique hour and minute hands might also provide at least a hint as to the maker's identification. As the front plate of the movement provides the most, but not all, of the distinctive clues as to the maker, gaining such a view is most helpful. However, this requires the removal of the bonnet from the case, then the hands from the dial and finally the dial from the movement. Generally speaking, only repairers, researchers or auctioneers choose to do this on a regular basis.

As we will be examining four extant Jones tall clocks, it can be presumed, and hoped, that additional examples exist but currently lack attribution.

Tall Clock #1

Our first tall clock example comes from the collection of the Ontario County Historical Society (OCHS) at Canandaigua, NY. The clock was donated to the Society in 1979 by a descendent of the Wheeler family of East Bloomfield. The *1820 Census* lists at least five Wheeler households in Bloomfield, including those of Twiney, Remember, Benjamin, John and George.[32]

Acquisition forms note that when the clock arrived at the Society it was disassembled, and when examined by the author it remained so in storage. The case and bonnet are together. The dial and pendulum were found in separate boxes, as was the movement. A smaller box held the key and pendulum bob. The original tin can weights and a "bag of assorted pieces of wood and string" rounded out the assemblage. The donor stated that the clock had been made at East Bloomfield by a "Robert Ham," but it is clearly the product of Abner and, now we know, Richard Jones.[33]

The cherry and tiger maple case of the OCHS clock (*see Figure 20*) is of interesting execution. The bonnet top is flat, a more outdated style than the arched pediments then fashionably found on most contemporary examples. The reeded molding running vertically up the sides of the bonnet is unusual while the reeding on the waist is not. Trim edging on the waist door is tiger maple. The case lacks feet, but it appears that an original base molding piece is missing so the original feet or base may be as well. All in all this is a very attractive country case in original finish. The maker of the case remains unidentified.

The decorated white enamel moon-phase dial is shown in *Figure 21*, and it may provide a clue as to the relative dating of the clock. The dial false plate (the dial posts pin to the false plate, which then pins into the movement, *see Figure 22*) is marked "Owen." Per clock historian Chris Bailey, the plate was manufactured at Birmingham, England, by Edward Owen, whose firm made components and tall clock dials from about 1800 until 1821. The painted dial itself has been identified by New England clock expert Paul Foley as dating from the period 1812-16 and having been produced at Boston by the firm of Nolan & Curtis, as the distinctive transfer printed hemisphere maps on the dial were only used on Boston dials.[34] Using the dial production dates, this might help place the clock as a "relatively early" Jones' product, and might suggest that the dials came with Abner and Richard when they left New Hampshire.

The movement from the OCHS clock is shown in *Figure 23*. The works carry the basic characteristics of all of the Abner/Richard and Abner Jones movements found in these clocks. One exciting discovery on the OCHS clock is the fact that the movement is numbered "7", the first documentation of such on a Jones New York tall clock (*see Figure 24*).

Figure 20

"Tall Clock #1" Cherry and
tiger maple case of the OCHS clock.

Figures 21 & 22

(Top) Dial back plate of the OCHS Jones tall clock
with the label of maker Edward Owen of
Birmingham, England, and (Bottom) dial.

The movements, like those of Jacob Jones but unlike those of most other American and English makers, feature the use of brass, other than the arbors, almost exclusively. On most movements of the period, the strike lifting pieces and rack and snail are of steel, while on the Jacob and Abner Jones clocks these parts are of brass. Abner Jones' clocks feature a screw adjustment on the bell hammer spring to soften or harden the bell strike (*see Figure 25*) and a round bell gong head (*see Figure 26*). The OCHS movement has a seconds bit and calendar function as reflected on the dial. The movement back plate and other clock components are shown in *Figures 27-30*.

While this entire clock was a wonderful find, the original cut-steel hands were of particular interest. As we shall see, most of the hands found on Abner Jones' clocks have a heart motif incorporated into the design. While this attribute has long been recognized in his shelf clocks, owing to the many more existing examples, this feature had remained unexamined in the Jones tall clocks until this study.

Chapter Two • 15

Figure 23

Front view of the 8-day brass movement found in the OCHS clock.

Figure 24

The OCHS tall clock has the number "7" stamped on the motion work on the front plate.

Figure 25

The screw-adjustable hammer spring attached to the back plate of the movement.

Photo Courtesy Tom Grimshaw

Figure 26

The rounded bell hammer casting found on all (except one, so far) of the Jones Bloomfield clocks.

Figure 27

Back plate of the OCHS tall clock movement.

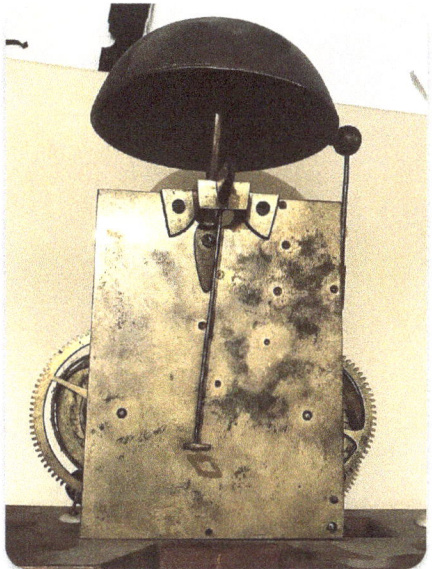

Figure 28

The wonderful original cut-steel hands.

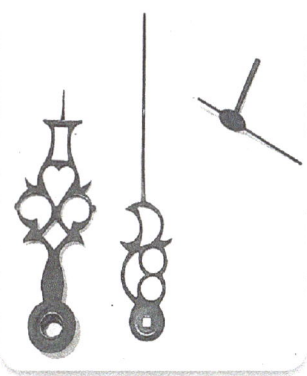

Figure 29

The interesting original pendulum bob.

Figure 30

The original tin can weights.

Tall Clock #2

Tall Clock #2 was featured in a Connecticut auction in 2015. All of the information was obtained by the author long after the sale so the extant photographs alone provide the basis for analysis. It appears possible that this is also an "early" example. As seen in **Figure 31**, the case, a clear departure from *Tall Clock #1*, is of a more traditional arched scroll top design, although here the scrolls are unusually delicate. The base case is cherry. Solid tiger maple is found on the bonnet columns and the reeded quarter columns on the waist. Tiger maple veneer strips decorate the waist above and below the quarter columns. The base and waist door are trimmed in mahogany and the center door panel is a remarkable cut of cherry. A horizontal strip of mahogany veneer runs along the top of the waist section below the bonnet and vertical strips of mahogany veneer run up the top of the bonnet sides and the center plinth and along the face edge of the scrolls. (*All photos of Tall Clock #2 courtesy Golden Gavel Auctions, LLC.*)

The dial (*see Figure 32*), is quite similar to that found on Tall Clock #1, and appears to be the work of Nolen & Curtis of Boston, circa 1815-20.[35] Features include a moon phase and calendar indicator and, importantly, the same distinctive cut-steel hands as on our initial tall clock.

As seen in **Figure 33**, the movement, while not examined in person and seen only obliquely in the auction offerings, can clearly be identified as a Jones product by the characteristics detailed previously, including the brass strike lifting pieces, the round bell hammer, and the adjustable hammer spring.

Figure 31

Case of the Jones Tall Clock #2 in cherry, tiger maple and mahogany.

Figure 32

Dial from Tall Clock #2, likely by Owen of Birmingham, England. Note the now-recognized distinctive "Jones" hands.

One extremely interesting feature of the case is found on the back of the door panel. In the midst of a long series of repair dates in pencil is a faint handwritten inscription which states: "*Made by Abner Jones/ Case Made by Daniel Miles/ Dec./1820.*" This information also shows up re-written, it would appear, at a later date, on the inside of the back board of the case. The latter reference is shown in **Figure 34**.

The next question is obvious – "Who was Daniel Miles?" Miles did not appear in the *1820 Census* for Bloomfield, NY, but was described as a resident in several property purchases in East Bloomfield in 1823. On March 12th of that year, he bought a house lot in the village from seller Daniel Buel. The lot? The exact one sold by Abner and Richard to Buel next to their own property in East Bloomfield in 1820.[36] However, Miles owned the lot for only a month before selling it and buying a commercial establishment on the Village Green called the "Farmer's Store." This would seemingly establish Miles as a general store owner/operator at that point. Miles did not appear in the *1830 Census*, but he was apparently still in East Bloomfield until 1836 when he sold the store to William Prindle and Isaac Mitchell. When that deed was signed, Miles was listed a resident of York, Livingston County, located approximately 25 miles west of East Bloomfield.[37]

One other potential casemaker, Simeon Deming, who was established at Bloomfield by 1813, will be discussed in **Chapter Seven**.

Figure 33

The Jones movement found in Tall Clock #2.

Figure 34

One of the two inscribed maker attributions found in the interior of Tall Clock #2. This, in pencil on the inside of the back board, appears to be a later duplicate of the faint pencil inscription found on the back of the center door panel. It reads: "Dec. 1820/ Made by Abner Jones/ Case made by Daniel Miles."

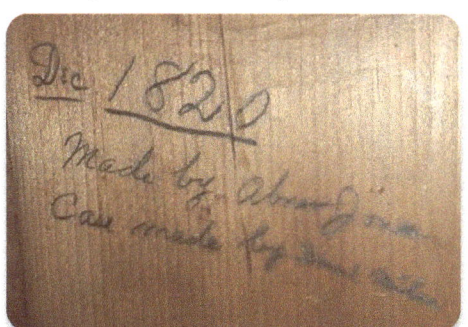

Figure 35

Jones tall clock with cherry case and arched scroll pediment.

Tall Clock #3

With the names of two possible Jones tall clock casemakers perhaps tantalizingly within reach, we have several other clocks for review and comparison. *Tall Clock #3* comes courtesy of Cottone's Auctions, Inc. of Geneseo, NY, and is a clock the gallery handled around 2009. **Figure 35** presents a full view of the clock, featuring a solid cherry case with a wonderful delicate arched scroll bonnet similar to, but not exactly like, that of *Tall Clock #2*. This dial (see close-up in **Figure 36**) features a seconds bit and calendar function but no moon phase, and appears to be an early William Jones, Philadelphia tall clock dial.[38]

Figure 36

Dial close-up from Tall Clock #3 with seconds bit and calendar but lacking a moon phase. The hands are duplicates of those found on Tall Clocks #1 and #2.

Figure 37

8-day Jones movement from Tall Clock #3.

The hands are duplicates of those found on *Tall Clocks #1 and #2*, as shown in **Figure 36**. The front plate of the movement from *Tall Clock #3* is shown in **Figure 37**. It should be noted that the movement seat board of this clock has a handwritten ink notation, in very small script, which states "*Abner Jones, Maker.*" Of course it is impossible to know whether this inscription dates back to the 1820s or is a more recent addition. (*All photos of Tall Clock #3 courtesy Cottone's Auctions, Inc.*).

Tall Clock #4

Our fourth tall clock comes courtesy of a long-time owner who sought information on the clock from the author in the 1980s. It is an wonderful case (***see Figure 38***) of cherry with mahogany veneer placed horzontally along the top of the waist section and vertically along the waist door edges and on the base panel center. It also has a scroll top pediment reminiscent of *Tall Clocks #2 and #3* in that the scrolls are very thin and delicate.

Like *Tall Clock #1*, the waist door is trimmed in tiger maple and while a different treatment, this waist section also has reeding on the sides, albeit on solid tiger maple quarter columns rather than a flat surface, just like *Tall Clock #2*. The bonnet columns are solid tiger maple and the base is also trimmed in tiger maple veneer. (*All photos of this clock courtesy Ken McHenry.*)

Pictures of the dial and movement from *Tall Clock #4* are shown in **Figures 39 and 40**, respectively. The dial is likely American by William Jones of Philadelphia.[39]

**Abner and Richard Jones –
Clockmakers in an Era of Change**

Even at the time Abner and Richard Jones left Pittsfield, NH, around 1818, the world of American clock making and marketing was fundamentally changing. The tradition followed by Abner and Richard's fathers was that of a handmade artisan trade specializing in producing the highest tier, and most exclusive, due to cost, clocks – the brass tall clock. The annual production total for many makers could be counted on a few hands. The world turned upside down during the years 1806-9 when the traditionally-trained Eli Terry of Plymouth, CT, (1772-1852) developed the vision and methodology to mass produce tall clock movements that ran 30 hours on a wind with interchangeable parts out of inexpensive wood rather than brass. His methods yielded clocks by the *thousands* per year, making this commodity suddenly and permanently accessible by "regular" households.[40]

After 1810, Terry retired, at least for a time, and set out to develop the next "big thing," a mass-produced weight-driven, wood works *shelf clock* movement.

Figure 38

Jones tall clock with cherry case and arched scroll pediment.

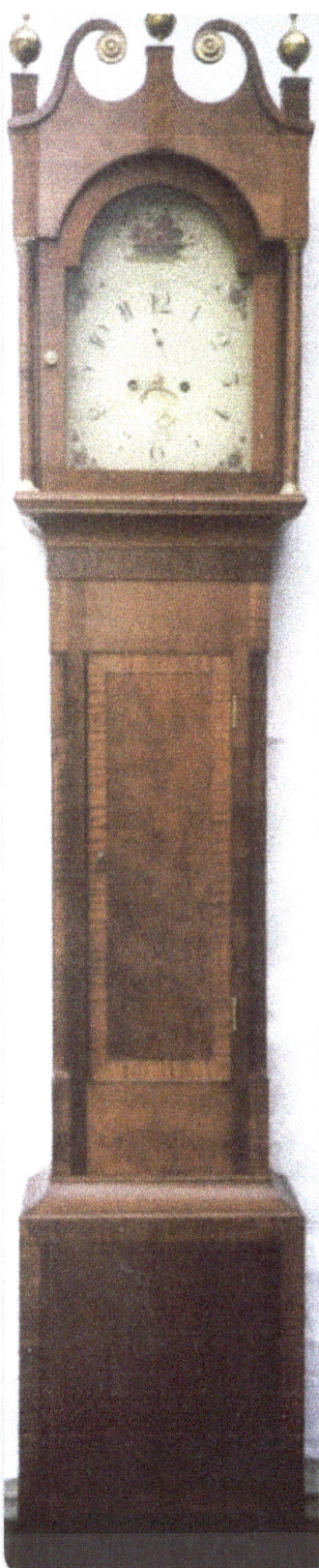

Figure 39

Close-up view of the dial of Tall Clock #4.

The numeral styles and simplified decorations on the dial indicate that this may be the product of maker William Jones of Philadelphia.

Note that these hands are of cast brass and clearly different from those found on Tall Clocks #1-#3. They appear to be old and nicely formed and may or may not be original to this clock.

Figure 40

Front plate of the Abner Jones movement from Tall Clock #4. As with Tall Clock #3, this movement features a seconds bit and calendar function.

Meanwhile, former workers and associates from his Plymouth factory, including Seth Thomas, Silas Hoadley, Riley Whiting, Joel Curtis and others set up their own factories using the Terry mass production methods, effectively sounding the death knell for the itinerant country clockmaker.[41] Between 1810 and 1820 these wood tall clocks were available throughout New England and peddlers reached into central New York State. Surely the warning signs, if not the actual demise, of traditional clock making was obvious to Jacob Jones and his son Abner; Joseph Jones and his son Richard.

So we have an informed rationale for Abner and Richard leaving New Hampshire for the then-western frontier — a chance to continue the trade they were born to, at least for a while. In just a few years, improved transportation routes and a rapid increase in population would make upstate New York an attractive and profitable ground for a new generation of peddlers of cheaper wooden gear clocks. For the pair, the years 1818 to the mid-1820s could be looked upon as a period of reprieve, but the year 1825 was pivotal. In that year the Erie Canal, the biggest public works project ever attempted by any state in the United States up to that point, was completed, establishing New York City as the commercial capital of the U.S.; opening up the Midwest and West to migration and development, and immediately opening up markets for agricultural and manufacturing producers in upstate New York to the national and world market.[42]

Suddenly, any clock producer in Connecticut could have his goods in the hands of dealers in upstate New York in a matter of weeks. A number of wood movement tall clockmakers, especially Riley Whiting of Winchester, CT, and Joel Curtis of Cairo, NY, set up distribution systems throughout upstate New York, and these reliable clocks could be sold at a fraction of the cost of a brass movement model.[43] The Jones' brass clocks, however well made, reliable and beautifully cased, simply could not compete. And yet by 1825 even the end of the *wood movement* tall clock era was in sight. The impetus came, again, from inventor Eli Terry, whose efforts to design a cheap, efficient 30-hour wood works *shelf clock* movement reached fruition by 1817. The movements were housed in attractive, fashionable "pillar and scroll" cases that were smaller, more practical and more transportable.[44] These clocks, too, were immediately marketed throughout upstate New York with the opening of the Erie Canal.

Evidence supports the assumption that Abner and Richard ceased tall clock production by 1828, and that their production partnership ended when Richard and family relocated at that time.

Richard Jones — 1828-46

At East Bloomfield, Richard and Lucy Ann Jones had three children, Joseph, Carlos and Lucinda. By 1828, the family had relocated to Springwater, Livingston County New York, approximately 25 miles southwest of East Bloomfield, where Richard reportedly continued in the foundry trade.[45] They did not record a deed for the property purchase at Springwater. Records indicate that their fourth child – John H. Jones – was born in July, 1828 at Springwater.[46]

The *1840 Census* shows Richard, Lucy and family living at Springwater, and Richard is listed as engaged in "manufacturing and trade." Richard died in 1846.[47] After his death, the family moved to Conesus, NY, where the 46-year-old Lucy and nine of her children living at home were recorded in the *1850 Census*.[48] The *1860 Census* recorded the family living at Geneseo, Livingston County and 33-year-old John H. and 26-year-old Myron W. Jones active in farming. In yet another link between the Abner and Richard Jones families, between 1860 and 1870, John H. Jones, son of Richard and Lucy, married Almira H. Jones, the daughter of Abner and Sabra.[49] By 1860 and thereafter until her death in 1890 at the age of 84, Lucy resided at the hamlet of Piffard, Town of York, Livingston County, NY, located just northwest of Geneseo. She was buried in the Temple Hill Cemetery, Geneseo, NY.[50]

[1] French, J.H. *Gazetteer of the State of New York*, Syracuse, NY,. R. Pearsall Smith, Pub., 1860, p. 496.

[2] Conover, George, Ed. *History of Ontario County, New York*, Syracuse, NY, D. Mason & Co., 1893, Chapter XXIII.

[3] Klien, D.B.: Majewski, J. "The Turnpike Movement in New York, 1797-1845," *Law and Society Review*, 1992, p. 469.

[4] Edwards, Evan. *Abner Jones Clockmaker*, (unpublished manuscript, August, 1982).

[5] Manke, Robert. *Genealogy of Abner Jones of Pittsfield*, (unpublished manuscript, November, 2018).

[6] *The Ontario Repository*, August 20, 1818, with thanks to Wesley Balla, Director of Collections and Exhibitions, New Hampshire Historical Society.

[7] Correspondence with Judi Stewart, East Bloomfield, NY, Historian.

[8] Edwards, Evan. Presentation Notes, Ontario County Historical Society, February 27, 1983.

[9] Beers, D.G. *Map of Ontario County, New York,1859*, A.R.Z. Dawson Publishing Co., Philadelphia, PA. 1859.

[10] *1820 U.S. Census* for Bloomfield, NY.

[11] Ontario County Deeds, Book 20, p. 151.

[12] Ontario County Deeds, Book 26, p. 463.

[13] *1810 U.S. Census and 1820 U.S. Census* for Bloomfield, NY.

[14] Ontario County Deeds, Book 46, p. 7.

[15] Ontario County Deeds, Book 46, p. 7; Book 46, p. 309; Book 53, p. 334.

[16] *1830 U.S. Census* for Bloomfield, NY, courtesy Robert Manke.

[17] Ontario County Deeds, Book 50, p. 413; Book 52, p. 323; Book 52, p. 322; Book 57, p. 372; Book 57, p. 442.

[18] *Ontario Repository and Freeman*, April 19 and 26, 1837, Courtesy Robert Manke.

[19] Correspondence with Robert Manke.

[20] *1820 U.S. Census* for Bloomfield, NY.

[21] Edwards, Evan. *Abner Jones Clockmaker*, (unpublished manuscript, August, 1982).

[22] *The Leading Citizens of Livingston and Wyoming Counties*. Biographical Review Publishing Co., Boston, MA, 1895, with thanks to Robert Manke.

[23] Ontario County Deeds, Book 38, p. 55.

[24] *1810 U.S. Census* for Bloomfield, NY

[25] French, p. 492.

[26] Ontario County Deeds, Book 59, p. 92.

[27] Ontario County Deeds, Book 59, p. 92.

[28] Ontario County Deeds, Book 38, p. 56.

[29] Walling, H.F. *1852 Map of Ontario County, New York*, Philadelphia, PA, 1852.

[30] Beers, D.G. *Map of Ontario County, New York, 1859*, A.R.Z. Dawson Publishing Co., Philadelphia, PA., 1859.

[31] *1820 U.S. Census* for Bloomfield, NY

[32] *1820 U.S. Census* for Bloomfield, NY

[33] Ontario County Historical Society Accession Record No. 1979.76.1.

[34] Personal Correspondence with Chris Bailey and Paul J. Foley.

[35] Personal Correspondence with Paul J. Foley, August 24, 2021.

[36] (Daniel Buel to Daniel Miles, Ontario County Deeds Book 41, pp. 541-2.

[37] *1820 U.S. Census* for Bloomfield, NY; Ontario County Deeds, Book 41, p. 541; Ontario County Deeds, Book 46, p. 7; Ontario County Deeds, Book 41, p. 540; Ontario County Deeds, Book 41, p. 539; Ontario County Deeds, Book 60, p. 167

[38] Personal Correspondence with Paul J. Foley, August 24, 2021.

[39] Personal Correspondence with Chris Bailey.

[40] Roberts, Kenneth and Taylor, Snowden. *Eli Terry and the Connecticut Shelf Clock*, Revised Second Edition. 1994, Ken Roberts Publishing Co., Fitzwilliam, NH, p. 50.

[41] Ibid., p. 60.

[42] For a comprehensive, engaging study of the Erie Canal and its impact on the New York and national economies, see Bernstein, Peter L. *Wedding of the Waters*, 2005, W.W. Norton & Co., New York.

[43] Oechsle, G. Russell and Boyce, Helen. *An Empire In Time: Clocks & Clock Makers of Upstate New York*. 2003, National Association of Watch & Clock Collectors, Inc., Columbia, PA, 2003.

[44] Roberts and Taylor. p. 98.

[45] *The Leading Citizens of Livingston and Wyoming Counties*. Biographical Review Publishing Co., Boston, MA, 1895, with thanks to Robert Manke.

[46] *Find a Grave.com*. Lucy Jones and family.

[47] *1840 U.S. Census* for Springwater, NY; *The Leading Citizens of Livingston and Wyoming Counties*. Biographical Review Publishing Co., Boston, MA, 1895.

[48] *1850 U.S. Census* for Conesus, NY.

[49] *1860 U.S. Census* for Livingston County, NY; Manke, Robert. *Genealogy of Abner Jones of Pittsfield* (unpublished manuscript November 2018).

[50] *Find A Grave.com*. Lucy Jones.

CHAPTER THREE

A New Enterprise – 1828-33

Abner Jones at Bloomfield

While at East Bloomfield, Abner and Sabra had two children who reached maturity, including Almira H., born in 1822, and William W., born in 1824.[1] As reviewed, the first home of Abner, Richard and their families was in the village of East Bloomfield. That homestead, rented or leased from Abner Adams, was sold by Adams in May, 1824. Evidence supports the fact that Richard Jones moved with his family to Springwater, Livingston County, NY, by 1828. The question of where Abner, Richard and their families lived after leaving their first Bloomfield home cannot, unfortunately, be definitively proven, as once again no deed records from the 1824-1828 period for the Joneses exist, suggesting, if not proving, that they once again rented a home after May, 1824.

Our best clue as to where Abner and Richard had relocated in 1824, and Abner and his family were in residence after 1828, comes from a study of the *1830 Census*. In 1830, Jones was a resident of the **town** of Bloomfield, appearing in the *Census* of that year along with **12** other enumerated members of the household. Accounting for the relative ages of Abner, Sabra and their three children, (Oliver C. was born in 1825), there are 8 additional, apparently unrelated, individuals listed, including 5 males and 3 females ranging from the ages of 15 through 29.[2] The evidence suggests that after their home in the village was sold in 1824, Abner and Richard leased or rented property and took up farming south of the village, and Abner remained there after Richard moved. Under this theory, the additional household members in 1830 could have been farm or foundry workers, or perhaps, as we will see, workers assisting Jones in beginning a new enterprise. While at their new home, Abner and Sabra added a fourth child, a son, Charles H., to the family in 1832.[3]

Lacking any deed references and any early maps that note the names of property owners, pinpointing the location of the new Jones homestead proved to be involved but ultimately productive. Taking into account the list of Abner's neighbors from the *1830 Census* and comparing it to property owners noted on the map of the town of East Bloomfield in 1852, one area of the town appeared promising.

The list of property owners living adjacent to Abner Jones in the *1830 Census* is noted below.[4] The individuals or family names underlined also appear on the 1852 map of the portion of the town of East Bloomfield shown in *Figure 41*. Assuming that the properties of William Steele and Elisha Wright were adjacent to the Abner Jones farm in 1830, a possible location of that homestead (owned by G.N. Parmelee in 1852) is circled in red.

A Portion of the Census List for the Town of Bloomfield, NY, – 1830

<u>Philo Hamlin</u>	Christopher Parks
<u>Thomas Kellogg</u>	Timothy Hubbard
<u>Elijah Hamlin</u>	Hamton (sp?) Joslin
Jonah Willson	<u>William Steele</u>
Nathan Wilson	Abner Jones
<u>Elisha Wright</u>	Nicholas West
<u>Jonathan Adams</u>	

Just to confuse things a bit further, the 1852 map does, in fact, list an *"A.Jones"* (highlighted in green on the map) just a short distance to the south and east from our presumed 1830 Abner Jones property. Some researchers have assumed that this was clearly the Abner Jones property, but alas, beginning in 1840, the *Census* records show that this was actually the farm of *Andrew* (or Andrus, which was likely just a misinterpretation by the census taker) Jones.[5] Andrew does not appear to have been related to Abner.

As noted above, the lack of a recorded deed in the mid to late 1820s for Abner Jones' new homestead might have been because he rented or leased the new property. That appears likely, as does Abner's determination to engage in farming at his new location, finally supported by the recorded purchase by Abner and Sabra Jones of a total of 108½ acres in three parcels in Lot #62 and one parcel in Lot #77 in Bloomfield from Flavius J. and Sally Bronson on January 7, 1832.

Figure 41

Adjacent property owners and presumed former Abner Jones homestead in Bloomfield as shown on the 1852 Map of Ontario County

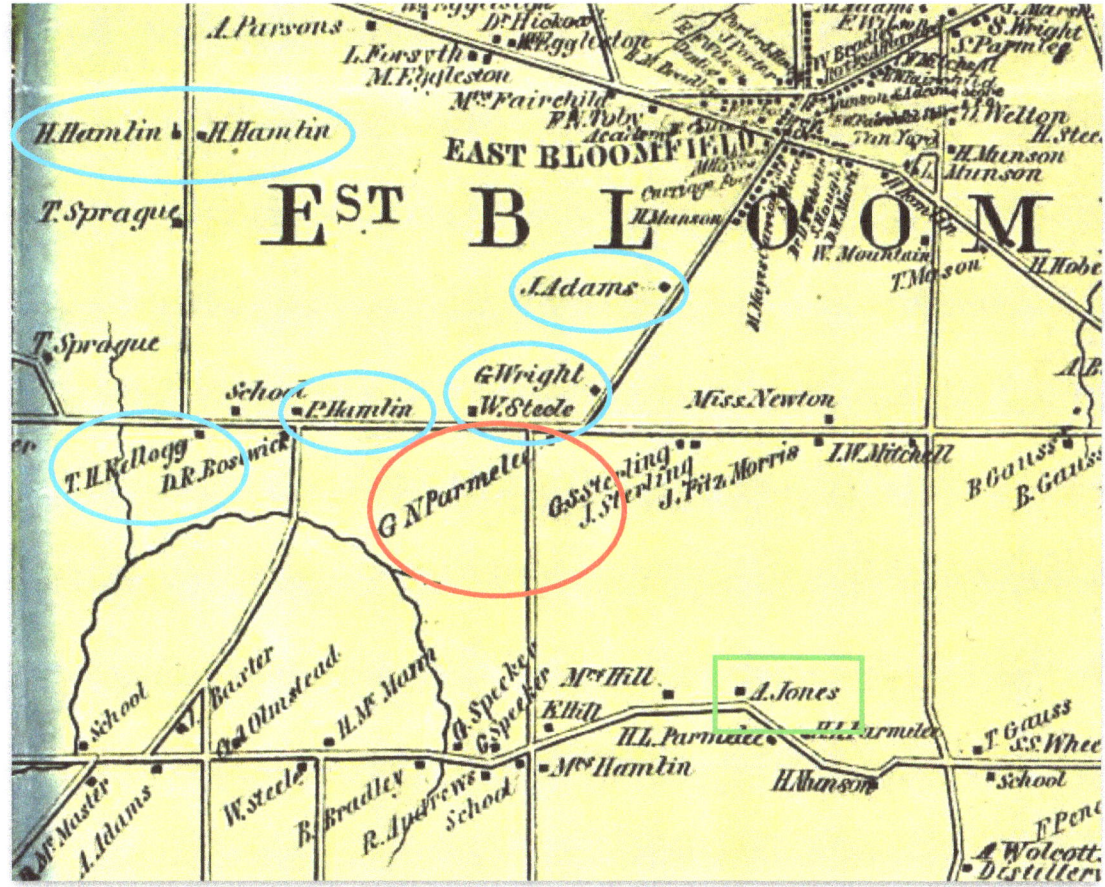

This transaction likely included the home the family had been living in. The full purchase price was $2,970, with Bronson giving a mortgage for the full amount.[6] The *1859 Map of Ontario County* is most helpful in illustrating where this property was, as that map edition includes the town lot lines. As shown in **Figure 42**, Lot #62 is where we supposed the Jones residence was located (owned by G.N. Parmele in 1852, shown owned in 1859 by "A. Cone"), and Lot #77 is directly south of Lot #62.[7]

On March 31, 1832, Abner and Sabra took a second mortgage for $1,500 from Evan Johns on the combined properties as purchased from Bronson.[8] Apparently this sum was borrowed to fully repay the first mortgage, which was recorded as discharged by Flavius Bronson on April 21, 1832.[9]

Figure 43 shows the Jones property and Lot #62 as it appears today looking north to south. The Jones homestead was at the circled area shown at the lower right area of the photo.[10]

Figure 44 shows the home at the site as it appears today.

Figure 42

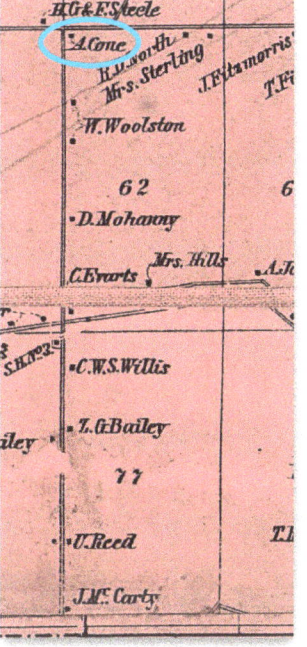

Lots #62 and #77, Town of East Bloomfield from the 1859 Map of Ontario County. The location of the Abner Jones homestead ca. 1828-35 is circled.

Chapter Three • 25

Figure 43

Modern aerial photo of the area occupied by Abner Jones as a homestead, foundry and farm of 108 acres in the early 1830s.

Google Earth photo

Figure 44

The home at the location of the Abner Jones homestead ca. 1830 as it appears today.

Clock Making Resumes in New and Distinctive Forms – 1831-1833

Were Abner Jones known only for his tall clocks, our story would be complete. In fact, however, he is hardly, if at all, historically known for his tall clocks and almost entirely recognized for a new enterprise inaugurated by 1831 – turning out remarkable shelf clocks unlike those produced by any other American maker. Facts and extant artifacts prove that far from being daunted by the forces that had destroyed the artisan brass movement tall clock trade in the 1820s, Abner Jones had, by 1831, decided to take advantage of economic, societal, interior design and marketing trends to reinvent himself as an 8-day brass movement shelf clockmaker. Prior researchers have identified a range of shelf clock production dates by Jones, most beginning, and ending, in the 1820s. The author hopes to produce evidence to better define these dates.

The factors that offered Abner Jones new clock making opportunities were several. First and foremost, the completion of the Erie Canal in 1825 was a huge boon to upstate New York merchants and producers. The nouveau riche of upstate New York revealed their new status by building stately Greek Revival homes with tall ceilings, massive fire places and rooms full of the latest "Empire-style" furniture. In contrast to the more delicate, austere styles of the Federal period, the Greek Revival and Empire fashions represented a new big, bold, independent ethic.[11]

Any home in the period needed a mechanical clock. Wealthy owners demanded exclusivity. By 1830 the Connecticut clock factories operating under the "American System" pioneered by Eli Terry were producing tens of thousands of clocks per year, but the vast majority were wood movement shelf clocks designed for the masses. Prior to 1830, brass movement 8-day shelf clocks were produced in small quantities and generally not marketed by peddlers outside Connecticut.[12] Even after 1830 Connecticut 8-day weight-driven brass movement clocks were slow to penetrate the upstate market. The individual who first identified the potential market for *locally-produced*, top-end, high-quality and high-priced 8-day shelf clocks in upstate New York was Asa Munger of Auburn, NY.

Munger was born at Granby, MA, in 1777 and apprenticed in the silversmith/goldsmith/clock making trade. After reaching maturity and producing a small number of wood and brass movement clocks at Ludlow, MA, he relocated to Herkimer, Herkimer County, NY, in 1803. At Herkimer, Munger operated a jewelry store and produced a small number of brass tall clocks before moving to the burgening new city of Auburn, Cayuga County by 1816. Once there, he resumed his jewelry store business, advertised "New Looking Glasses Just Received from the Utica Factory" and, somewhat less prominently, "Brass eight day clocks made by his own hand."[13]

What were perhaps Munger's earliest products at Auburn were the type of clock shown in **Figure 45**. These substantial clocks combined Federal mirror and Empire styles and were designed to be placed on a mantel or wall. These early clocks featured unique 8-day *timepiece* movements (i.e., the clocks just told time; no strike feature was included) (*see Figure 46*), with brass gears and pewter plates to save on costs. After several years of experimentation, Munger settled on one basic case style, shown in **Figure 47**, and the vast majority of these housed his unique 8-day brass time-and-strike movements (*see Figure 48*). At around 40" tall, these clocks were a formidable presence on the mantel in an owner's parlor.[14]

With Munger shelf clocks having circulated for over a decade, by 1830 Abner Jones must have known of and seen his products. Clearly, Munger had identified a niche market unmet in upstate New York by the Connecticut makers. Abner Jones apparently made the determination to throw his hat in as Munger's first serious upstate competitor.

Asa v. Abner

For both Asa Munger and Abner Jones, market demand dictated many features of their clocks. Within that context, they were able to act with significant creativity. Wealth and prestige dictated that the clock movements be of brass and meet the 8-day running standard. The brash new Greek Revival architecture and Empire furniture styles required similar attributes in their clocks, and the scale of the settings meant the clocks needed to be sized in kind. Collectors also often note similarities between the Munger and Jones clocks, but mostly their clocks were similarly big, of high quality, beautiful and expensive.

The Abner Jones Chronology

While Abner Jones shelf clocks in their many variations have long been appreciated by owners and collectors, divining an accurate chronology of case styles and production has never been attempted. This work will endeavor to use the evidence as presented by the extant Jones shelf clocks to lay out a reasonable timeline. Abner will deliver again with a few tantalizing, but not nearly definitive enough, clues. The author will attempt to put them in a semblance of order, all of which will suffice until a better investigator comes along.

We Take All the Clues We Can Get

Those familiar with Abner Jones shelf clocks are aware of one oft-repeated statement: *"Abner Jones produced about 100 clocks."* Jones did number (some of) his clock movements and, with one exception, as we will see, no numbers to date exceed the magic 100 threshold. The problem is that *he didn't number all of his clocks!* An effort to create a chronology of case styles and production would be simplified if every clock had a number, but in fact only a bit more than a third of the extant Abner Jones shelf clocks are so inscribed. Various theories have been put forth to explain why a maker would number some of his production but not all. In the end, hoping that a sound theory would overcome speculation has proven to be futile, and we are left to deal with the evidence we have as best we can.

In addition to *some* clocks having numbers, *some* of the clock movements are *dated*. This group of clocks represents an even smaller sample size, but this is nonetheless a wonderful clue and, when combined with the clocks with numbered movements, serves as our primary basis for determining case design chronology.

What Came First?

Contrary to previous speculation, **1830-31** appears to be the time period when Abner Jones began his shelf clock production, and the evidence comes in an unexpected form – an 8-day brass movement *timepiece* unlike any other Jones shelf clock found to date. As a single known example, the movement could be considered a short-lived experiment. The singular subject clock is shown in **Figure 49**. This clock is full of curiosities set to amaze and confound the researcher and collector. We will deal with each element of the clock individually, as each is significant to our understanding of later Jones cases and movements.

The Group One Clocks

For review purposes, the case style represented in **Figure 49** will be termed as part of **Group One**. All of the Jones shelf clocks with early dates and numbers appear in this style case. As the earliest dated shelf clock, this example will be identified as *Clock 1-A*.

The case is pine with solid and veneer mahogany. The **height of the case measures 39". Width at the base is 18⅝", width of the upper case is 15" and width of the top cornice board is 21½". Depth at the base is 7", at the upper case 6½", and depth of the top board is 8¾".**

The dimensions of Clock 1-A are typical of all of the Group One cases we will examine, but these cases were clearly made one at a time, so the cases in this group can and do vary up to ½" in each individual dimension.

Figure 45

Early Asa Munger 8-day timepiece in a solid birdseye maple case emulating the mirror, or "looking glass" styles of the late 1810s.

Figure 47

Asa Munger, Auburn, NY, clock. From the early 1820s through 1830, this was the basic clock produced by Munger for his wealthy clientele.

Figure 46

Munger's earliest clocks featured these unique 8-day timepieces with pewter plates and brass gears.

Figure 48

Unique 8-day brass time-and-strike movement used by Munger in most of his clocks.

Figure 49

Abner Jones 8-day brass movement timepiece numbered "150", dated "1831".

Chapter Three • 29

The case can best be described as "heavy Empire" with its paw feet, huge cornice top and substantial column treatment. A feature virtually unique to the Abner Jones shelf clocks is a lower "cabinet" section with multiple drawers. As with Asa Munger's standard cases, the doors of Abner's **Group One** cases feature a large "looking glass," an attractive and valuable accessory in clocks of this period.

Clock 1-A has four drawers in the cabinet base, one full-width with rounded front, and three upper drawers, each measuring 5" wide, 3" high and 6¾" deep. The two flanking upper drawers and the lower drawer have glass pulls, and the upper middle door is key closure only. The pulls on *Clock 1-A* are obvious replacements. Standard pulls will be examined on other **Group One** clocks. The sides of the upper case on this clock are rounded.

Group One dials exhibit features not found on later Jones clocks, including the hand styles, chapter ring dimensions and numeral styles. The dial from *Clock 1-A* is shown in **Figure 50**.

Abner Jones' shelf clock dials are unique, consisting of two parts: a circular, unadorned inner dial (other than by seconds bits on some) attached by pillar posts to the movement, and a square outer dial with an open center, chapter ring, numerals, minute marks and decorated spandrels *attached to the back of the upper door*, thus opening with the door.

Figure 50

Dial format of Clock 1-A, *showing the gilt chapter ring approx. 7/8" wide, Arabic "open" script numerals, hand-painted floral decorations in the spandrels and minute markers on the inside circle of the dial, made necessary by Abner Jones' unique treatment where the outer dial is attached to the door and the inner dial to the movement.*

Figures 51 & 52

The back views of the cast zinc dials from Clock 1-A.

Figure 53

A Jones outer dial attached to the back of the case door.

Both dials are of cast zinc, and the use of zinc as the dial material clearly presented problems for retaining paint. This will be a consistent issue with Abner's dials, but observations appear to indicate that in general, the primer and paint on the **Group One** clocks, such as the pristine original dial of *Clock 1-A*, has held up much better over the last 200 years than those in some later groups. The backs of the cast zinc dials from *Clock 1-A* are shown in **Figures 51 and 52**, and **Figure 53** shows an outer dial attached to the inside of a Jones shelf clock door.

The original hands found on *Clock 1-A* support the notion that **this may be the original shelf clock prototype**. *These hands are unlike those found on any other Abner Jones shelf clock, but yet are absolutely identifiable as his product because they are a set of his tall clock hands, cut down to fit the shorter dimensions required by the diameter of the shelf clock's inner dial.* **Figures 54 and 55** show a set of Jones tall clock hands and the cut-down set found on Clock 1-A, respectively. The use of the cut-down tall clock hands resulted in a rather ungainly dial appearance. Abner must have felt the same way. All of his other shelf clocks would have different hands. When the author first saw pictures of this clock, he told the owner that the hands were clearly not original. The author eventually got smarter.

As noted, *Clock 1-A* has rounded sides on the central case and a rounded front on the lower, full-length drawer. Variations among other **Group One** clocks will be noted as appropriate.

All **Group One** clocks identified to date have turned pine columns. Some columns are painted, some gilt, some painted and stenciled, some stained. We will review differences as each clock is examined. With respect to *Clock 1-A*, it is the only **Group One** example found to date with turned columns painted black with no other decoration. A close examination indicates that this clock never had stenciling, and the current finish absolutely appears original. In addition, while each of the Group's clocks has turned columns, the exact turning on *Clock 1-A* is shared with only one other clock, identified and compared for our purposes as *Clock 1-B*.

Figure 54

Abner Jones tall clock hands.

Figure 55

The cut-down tall clock hands found on shelf Clock 1-A.

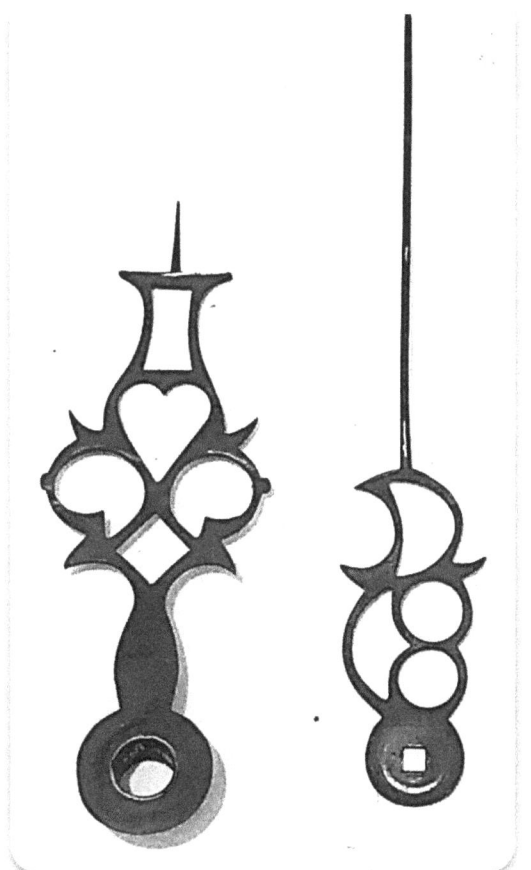

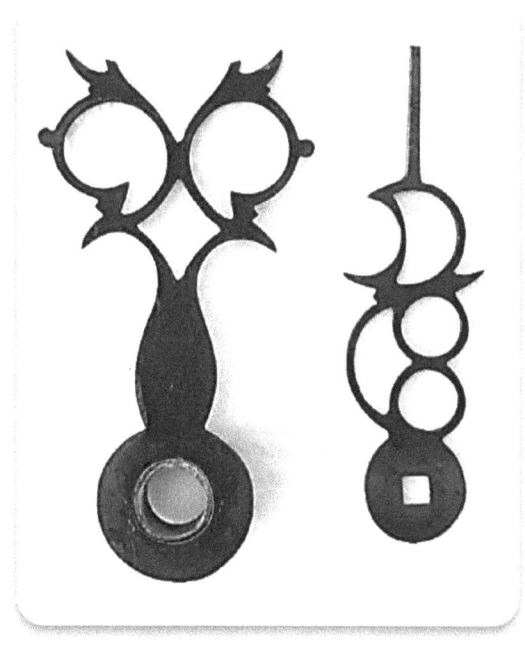

Chapter Three • 31

Figure 56 & 57

Figures 56 (below left) and 57 (below right):
Showing the Abner Jones timepiece movement front and side views, respectively.

The Timepiece Movement

The timepiece movement front and side views are shown in *Figures 56 and 57*.

This is a four-wheel, time-only movement measuring approximately 5" high, 3" wide and 2½" deep. The pendulum is suspended from a stud on the back plate of the movement, and the back plate of the movement is attached to wood spacer strips on each side, which, when the strips are screwed to the back board of the case, provide clearance for the pendulum.

As shown obliquely in *Figure 57* and in a close-up in *Figure 58*, the front right side of the back plate is stamped "**1831**." This is the earliest date inscribed on any Abner Jones shelf clock.

The movement yields yet another surprise. On the back of the back plate, under the wood spacer strip on the right side is a movement number. As shown in *Figure 59*, the number is "**150**." This picture was taken the day the author initially examined the clock and had his first opportunity to contemplate the meaning of the number prior to the cleaning of the movement. The moment was memorable.

Figure 58

The "1831" date stamped on the timepiece.

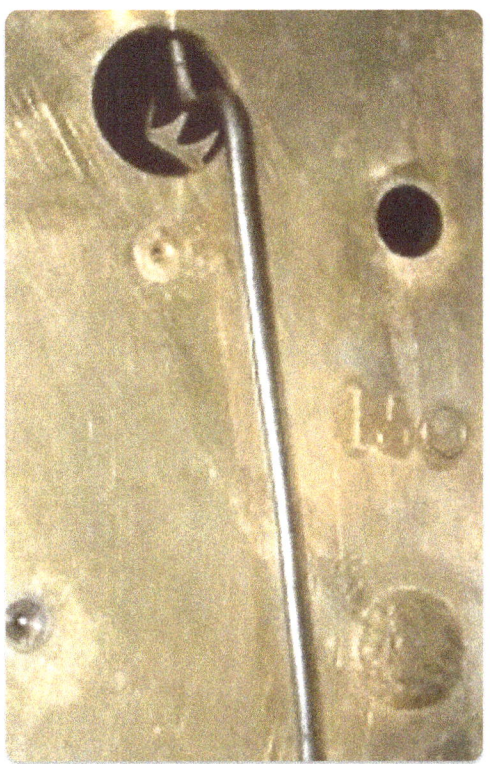

Figure 59
The number "150" stamped on the back of the back plate of the timepiece movement.

As we all "knew," no Abner Jones shelf clocks had been found with a number over 100," but here was a clock and movement with the earliest known production date by year but yet the highest number seen. What did it mean? A simple answer was offered by the late Snowden Taylor, one of the foremost horological researchers of the last 50 years. Given the facts, Snowden speculated, "Well, he was starting a separate number series for timepiece movements; different from the time-and-strike clocks." No one has given a more plausible explanation to date, so consider it accepted!

The Nominee for Clock 1-B

No time-and-strike shelf clock number "1" has been found, but the author has a nominee. *Figure 60* shows an Abner Jones shelf clock case with dimensions essentially the same as *Clock 1-A* as well as the other **Group One** clocks we will examine. The sides are rounded, and the cabinet section incorporates drawers, although three, not four. The drawers have appropriate glass pulls. The dial is excellent and original and *of the same overall pattern as Clock 1-A*, albeit with a seconds bit insert. Like *Clock 1-A*, this dial has open script numerals. *Only Clock 1-A and this clock appear with open script numerals*, and there is one additional unique similarity, and one meaningful difference.

CLOCK 1-A: THE BACK STORY

In the process of researching this book, some wonderful clock histories have come to light and these will be presented with the respective clocks. Clock 1-A has, for virtually all of its life, been owned by male members of the Fitch family. The clock was first sold to Joshua Fitch of Bristol, Ontario County. Fitch's farm at the time was approximately 5 miles due south of Abner Jones's 1830 homestead. The clock resided with Joshua at Bristol into the mid-1850s after which Joshua and son Horace moved to Rushville, Ontario County. Joshua died in 1859 and Horace inherited the clock. When Horace passed away in 1873, the clock went to his son Walter R. at Rushville. When Walter died in 1924, the clock was inherited by his son Horace W., who was to become a highly respected Ontario County Judge at Canandaigua, NY. With Horace W.'s passing in 1947, his son Walter Miller Fitch of Wichita, KS, took possession of the clock and, by 2005, it resided with Walter's son Ross Andrew Fitch in Kansas. It is fascinating to think of the clock being passed down over the years with such care and affection from generation to generation, and for the clock to have survived in such original condition.[15]

Figure 60

The shelf clock designated 1-B due to its close similarities to Clock 1-A.

34 • *Without Equal: The Clocks of Abner Jones of Bloomfield, New York*

While all of the **Group One** clocks have *turned columns*, the columns on only one other clock, **this one**, match the *exact* turnings found on *Clock 1-A*, which would imply similar construction dates. Instead of black paint, these columns are wonderfully gilt. Based on this accumulation of evidence, the author hereby anoints this example as his choice for *Clock 1-B*.

The turned columns from *Clocks 1-A and 1-B* are shown in *Figure 61* for comparison purposes. With apologies for the slight differences due to the focal distance of the pictures, the turnings on both sets of columns are the same.

Our last comparison involves the dial hands. As noted, the timepiece has modified tall clock hands. Different cut-steel hands, unique and very attractive, appear on *Clock 1-B*. The minute hand, hour hand and seconds bit indicator are shown in *Figure 62*.

These hands incorporate the heart and half-moon motifs found on Jones' tall clock hands in a new combination. The seconds bit indicator hand is especially pleasing with its central heart shape. These exact designs are, so far, found on no other Abner Jones shelf clock, and may point to this version as being an early prototype.

Figure 61

Showing the comparison between the turned columns on Clocks 1-A and 1-B.

Figure 62

The distinctive – and unique – cut-steel hands found on Clock 1-B.

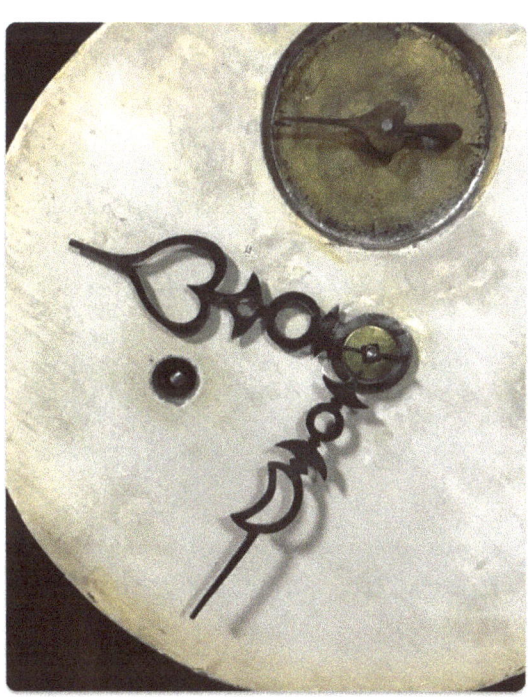

The New-Old Movement

After, or along with, his experimental timepiece, Abner Jones reverted to a tried-and-true form – his time-and-strike brass, 8-day tall clock movement – to adapt for use in his shelf clocks. With modifications to most of the gear wheel tooth and some of the pinion leaf counts, the pendulum length could be reduced to fit in the shorter shelf clock case, and with compounding, the weights would supply power for 8 days. The new pendulum length required a case height of approximately 26". Even at that, most cases required a bit of gouging in the wood base board to accommodate the end of the pendulum rod and the rating nut. A "typical" (*not the movement from Clock 1-B*) shelf clock movement is shown in *Figures 63 and 64*.

Figure 63

Front view of a typical Abner Jones shelf clock movement, a modified version of his time-and-strike tall clock movement.

Figure 64

Time side view of the typical Jones shelf clock movement. The circle indicates the space on the front of the back plate where most movement numbers, when they exist, are found.

Figure 65

Back plate view of a typical Abner Jones shelf clock movement. Note the wood spacer strips and back plate cutout.

With several exceptions, which will be noted as they appear, when a number is stamped on an Abner Jones movement, it appears on the *front of the back plate on the time side of the movement between the top of the great wheel and the upper right plate pillar post*. Most, but not all, Jones shelf clock movement back plates have cutouts of various shapes in the lower middle area to facilitate the placement of the pendulum rod on the suspension bracket (***see Figure 65 and further detail in Chapter Ten***).

So with its case anointed, for the moment at least, as potentially the first one produced with a time-and-strike movement, what of the movement from *Clock 1-B*? Well, the movement absolutely is numbered, just not with a "1" or a "2." Remarkably, and ironically, it is inscribed with *the highest number yet found on an Abner Jones shelf clock movement - 96*. In **Chapter Eight** we will examine the type of case a movement with this high number might otherwise have appeared in, but for now we will contemplate just when and where the movement swap — if there was one — took place. If this case originally contained the first time-and-strike shelf clock movement, did that mechanism fail after just a few years and a later replacement installed? Was the movement damaged over the years and a loose movement found to replace it? Or was something more remarkable taking place?

When the current owner obtained this clock, the movement shown was in the case, appearing perfectly original. Had an exchange of movements taken place, it would not have been difficult, as Abner's shelf clock movements remained virtually unchanged over the years. A number of the late-run clocks featured dials with seconds bits, so fashioning a replacement movement to the original dials seemingly would have posed no problem.

The conundrum deserves a full airing. Where does the evidence take us? First, this *does appear to be a late production movement*. Along with the number "**96**" found in the "usual" place on the right front face of the back plate of this movement, an additional number – "**17**"– appears on the lower center front of the back plate, just left of the edge of the time side great wheel. Setting aside, at least for the moment, what "**17**" might mean, we must also contemplate the fact that there exists a late Abner Jones cornice and carved column shelf clock with a movement numbered "**95**" in the "usual" position that has the number "**16**" also stamped on the center lower edge of the front of its back plate *(see Chapter Eight)*. Such double sequencing of production numbers would appear to clearly establish movement "**96**" *as a late production movement*.

Does this establish the "failed movement" replacement theory as most likely? Under other circumstances it probably would, but Abner Jones repeatedly surprises us and here we have another example, for the number "**96**" movement is anything but standard. Rather, it is, among extant Abner Jones shelf clocks, simply unique, making it seem at least possible that Jones put *that* movement in *this* case on purpose. *Figures 66-72* give us a reason to believe.

Figure 66 provides a side view of the strike train gears between the plates of *Clock 1-B*. The photo offers a fantastic tableau of turned pillar posts and collets (the brass collars securing the gears to the steel arbors) in almost fairyland shapes. The "normal" Abner Jones shelf clock movement is as well made and finely finished as any American shelf clock of the period. The embellishments found on movement #96 take the standard movement to another level and beyond. For comparison, **Figure 67** shows a view of the same gears from the time side of a "typical" Abner Jones movement.

Figures 68 and 69 provide close-up views of the gears seen in **Figure 66**. The back plate, minus gears, is shown in *Figure 70*. It may be interesting to note that the cutout in the back plate on this clock is circular, a form not seen to date on any other Jones clock. **Figures 71 and 72**, respectively, show the stamped numbers "**96**" and "**17**" located on the back plate.

The singular combination of *Clock 1-B* becomes utterly compelling. The evidence to date linking one of the earliest of Abner Jones' shelf clock cases with one of his last, but absolutely special and unique, over-the-top, movements cannot simply be coincidence. The author is tempted to speculate that this was a clock that Jones kept in his possession, at least for a while, and for very personal reasons. While we await the divine delivery of definitive answers, we will gratefully enjoy the beauty of the clock and the expert craftsmanship of its maker.

CLOCK 1-B: THE BACK STORY

As with Clock 1-A, *our current clock has a wonderful back story; one not subject to conjecture, because an ink-on-linen-paper written history came with the clock in an envelope placed in the lower full drawer of the case. The letter was written on September 15, 1937, by an elderly grandmother to her granddaughter, who was expecting a child. In passing the clock down she related that the clock had always been in the Wilder family, from Joseph [resident of Bristol, NY, in 1830]; to his son Erastus, and that her wish was that "the old Wilder clock and that name is preserved by each inheritor thereafter." Tracking the family line using modern Ancestry.com resources, it appears that the writer was likely Julia Wilder Webster (1872-1943) of Hilton, NY. She goes on to relate how she had received the clock years earlier: "When it was sent to me from N. York the box in which it came was packed with dried apples in and around it in every space to hold [the clock] firmly. It was not injured in the least. Furthermore, the dried fruit was of choice [eatable] winter apples thus making an additional contribution much appreciated."[16]*

Figure 66

View between the plates, strike side, of the remarkable movement of Clock 1-B. Consider the work required to turn the collets (the collars securing the gears to the steel arbors) in these intricate shapes. The pillar posts (left corner of the movement) also receive extra turnings on this movement.

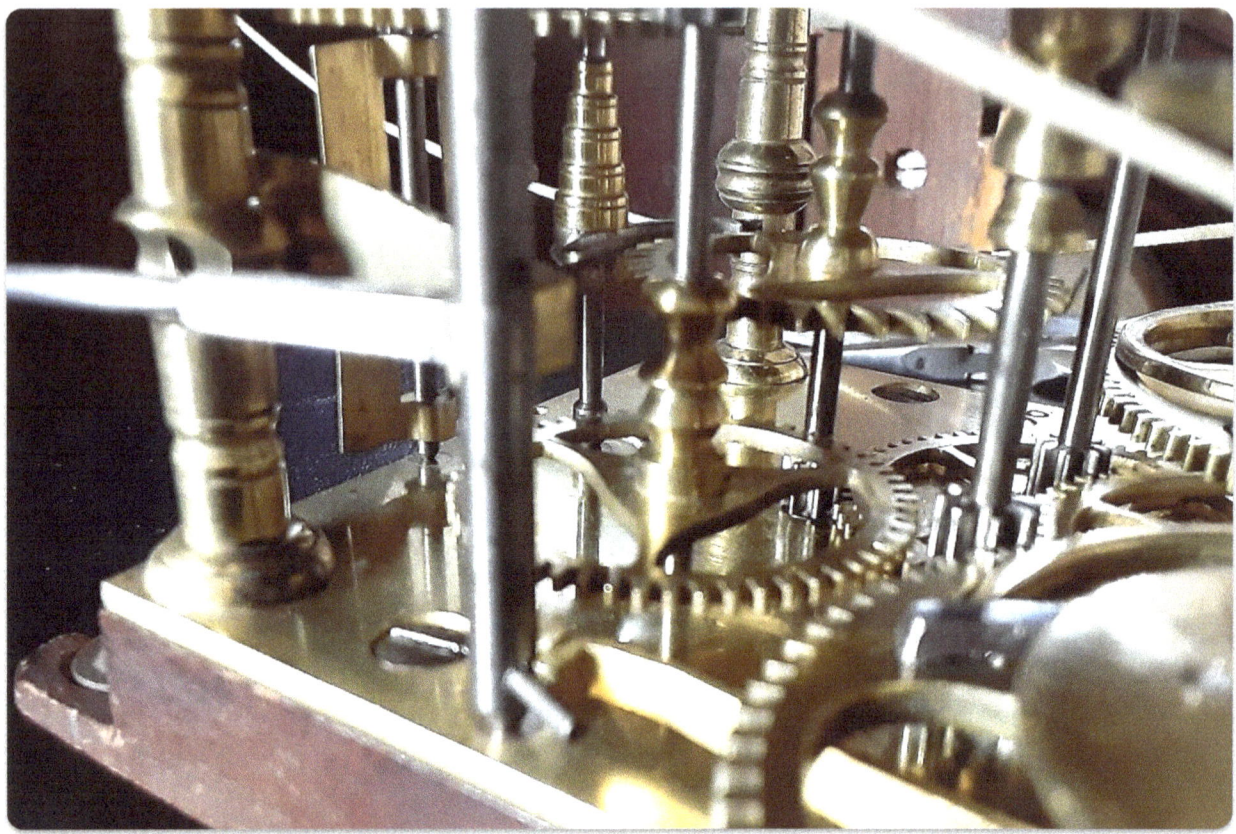

Photo Courtesy Tom Grimshaw

Figure 67

A "standard" Abner Jones movement as viewed from the time side for comparison with the extra workmanship found on Clock 1-B above.

Figures 68 & 69

Figures 68 (top) and 69 (bottom) showing the remarkable workmanship on the gears in Clock 1-B.

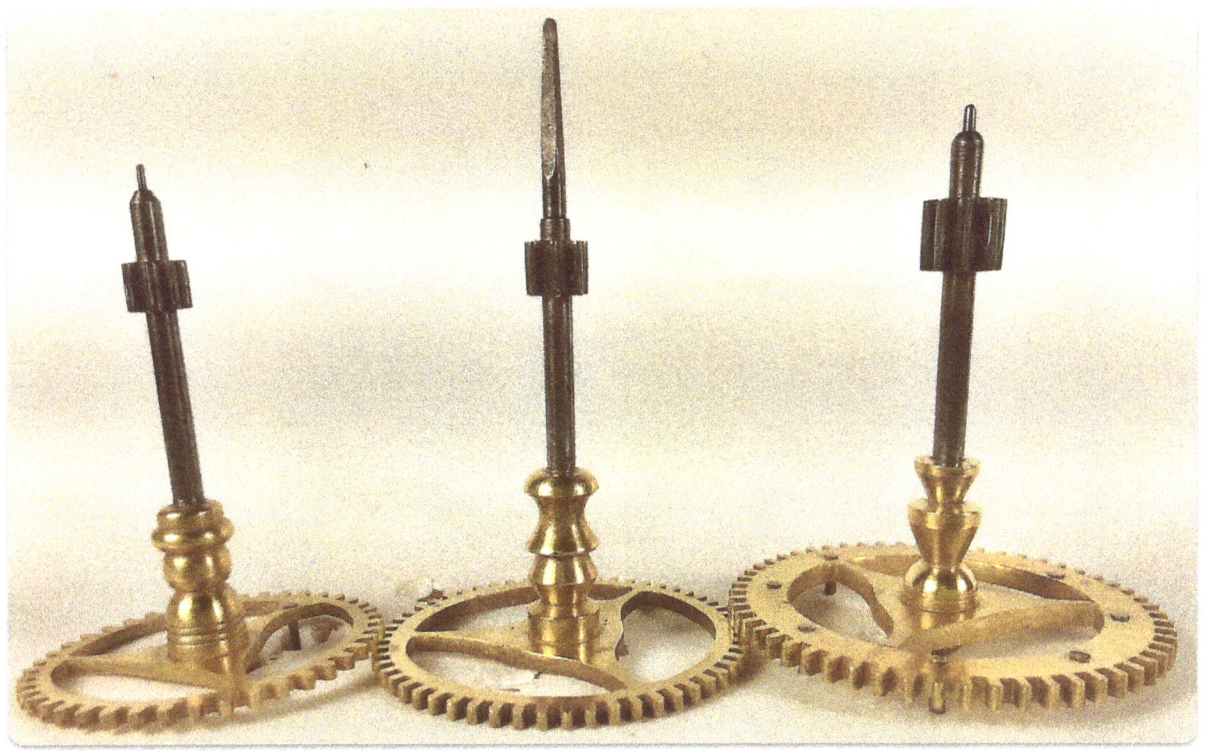

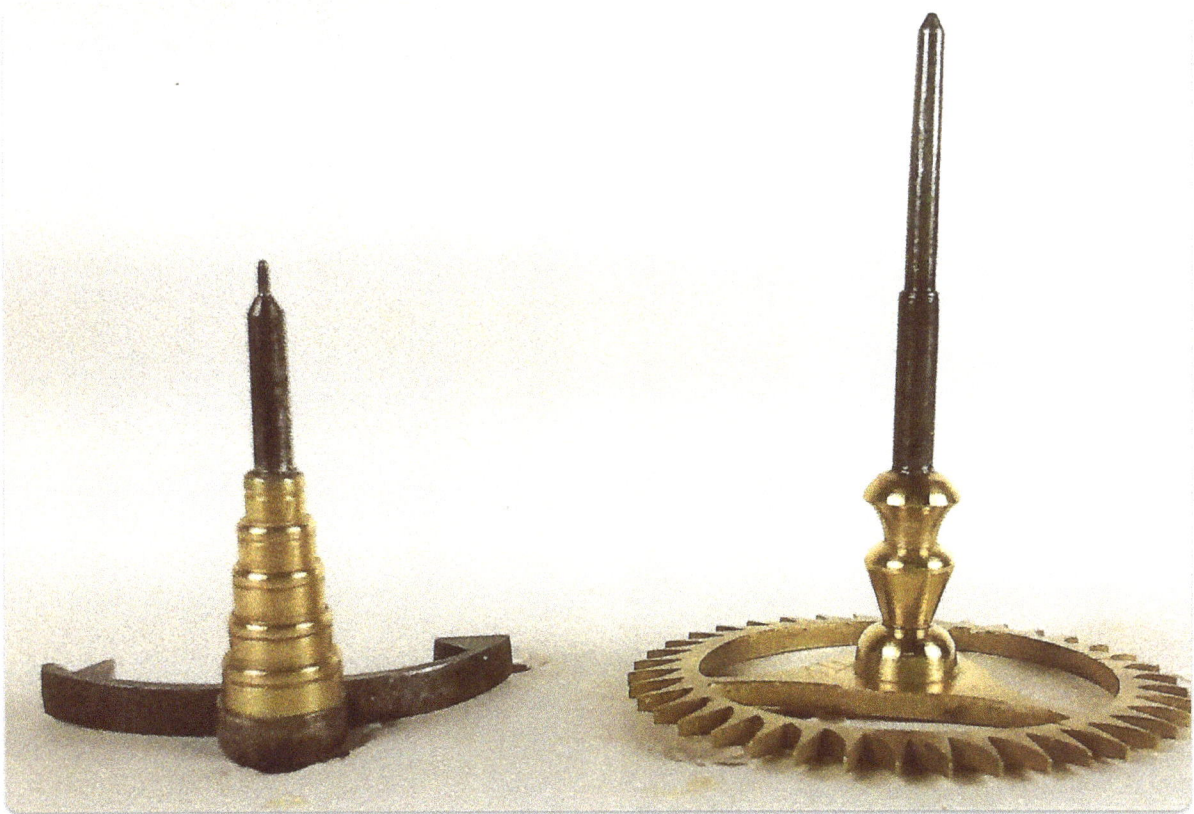

Photos Courtesy Tom Grimshaw.

Chapter Three • 39

Figure 70

View of the exposed inside back plate of Clock 1-B. The circular cut-out form on this back plate has not been seen on any other Abner Jones shelf clocks to date.

Photo Courtesy Tom Grimshaw

Figures 71 & 72

Figures 71 (left) and 72 (right) showing the numbers found stamped on the back plate of Clock 1-B.

Photos Courtesy Tom Grimshaw

A Clock Numbered "2"

Half of the identified **Group One** (early) Abner Jones shelf clocks have numbered movements, one of the highest proportions of any of the case types. One of those cases has a movement stamped with the **number "2."** This clock, identified as *Clock 1-C*, is shown in **Figure 73**. Once part of the notable clock collection of Herb Nilson of Atrim, NH, it is now in a private collection in New York State.

This case features natural wood columns in a *new turned pattern* with rosettes on the lower blocks. The case features a three-drawer cabinet base like *Clock 1-B*, but with a *lower drawer with a flat front*. Also flat are the case sides. This is the first, but not the last, case with these features. The drawer pulls are replacements for the original glass pulls.

While the gilt chapter ring is the same width as those on our first two examples, the gilt decorative ring circling the chapter ring is gone, which leaves a noticeable void between the chapter ring and spandrels, and the minute ring is now also gilt. This and several subsequent clocks retain a new cut-steel hand design, a better picture of which is presented in **Figure 77**. The movement number on this clock is stamped onto the upper right edge of the *front plate*, as shown in **Figure 74**.

Clocks 1-A and 1-B have weight pulleys *internal* to the case. On *Clock 1-C* the pulleys are incorporated into the top board. They can be seen protruding from the top of the clock in **Figure 73**.

A Clock Numbered "3"

The clock designated as "1-D" is shown in **Figure 75**. This case has the same column turnings as *Clock 1-C*, but in this instance they are painted black with original stenciling. The case sides are rounded, as is the front of the lower cabinet drawer. The drawers feature original glass pulls. The dial treatment on this clock is the same as *Clock 1-C*, and this clock features the new cut-steel hand patterns first seen on *Clock 1-C* (*see Figure 77*). The inner dial features a gilt second bit and a simple pointer hand.

Figure 76 shows the inside front of the back plate of the movement of *Clock 1-D* and the stamped number "**3**".

Clock 1-D has one other distinction – it is the first of a number of Jones shelf clocks with wallpaper lining on the inside of its case. Sealing the inside of a clock case with wallpaper was a notable feature of Asa Munger's clocks produced at Auburn, NY, as well as the successor firm of Hotchkiss & Benedict (active 1833-36). Ostensibly, the wallpaper sealed the interior from dust, but in terms of practicality it seems more intended for decorative effect. Munger's wallpaper tended to be quite colorful and varied, whereas with one exception, all of the wallpaper found in extant Jones' shelf clocks has the same pattern, and the use of this one pattern was, based on clocks seen to date, limited only to Group One and, as we will see, Group Two cases. The wallpaper in *Clock 1-D* is especially water stained, so a better example will be shown below.

― *Figure 73* ―

Clock 1-C *contains a time-and-strike movement stamped with the number "2".*

Photo Courtesy Skinner's Auctions, Inc.

― *Figure 74* ―

Front plate of the movement of Clock 1-C *showing the location of the stamped number "2".*

Figure 75

Jones shelf clock designated as 1-D. The movement in this clock is stamped "3," and the case shows a number of similarities with Clock 1-C.

Figure 76
The movement of Clock 1-D stamped with the number "3."

Figure 77
The new cut-steel pattern found on the hands of Clocks 1-C and 1-D.

A Clock Numbered "6"

The clock with the time-and-strike movement stamped with the number "**6**" and the date "**1832**" is now in the museum collection of the National Association of Watch & Clock Collectors, Inc. (NAWCC) at Columbia, PA. The clock was donated for this purpose by the long-time owners, the Baker family of West Bloomfield, NY, and was repaired, refurbished and delivered to Columbia by members of the NAWCC Western New York Chapter #13 (*see Back Story below*). This clock, designated 1-E, is shown in **Figure 78**.

CLOCK 1-E: THE BACK STORY

The first owner Clock 1-E was Jasper Gideon Baker (1800-1854), son of Bayze Baker, a pioneer settler of West Bloomfield, NY. Family history suggests that the clock was a wedding present and that it cost $30 or $40 at that time. Following Jasper Baker's death, the clock was inherited by his second wife Persis Hughes Baker (1836-1871) then to son Ortes Baker (1841-1902). After Ortes' passing the clock went to his daughter Marion Baker Green (1880-1948). Marion's sister Jeannette (1845-1910) married into the Griffith family and Marion's niece Cora Louise Griffith Parrish (1864-1933) was the next caretaker of the clock. After Cora's death the clock went to her daughter Hazel Parrish White (1894-1969). After Hazel's passing the clock was being shared among her children when they jointly made the decision to preserve the clock in a museum where members of the public could see "tangible evidence of the skill and diligence of early Western New York settlers and... the foresight of the Baker family who valued and carefully preserved the clock down through nearly 150 years." The family contacted Evan Edwards in the late 1970s with their intentions, and with his help and that of other members of NAWCC Western New York Chapter 13, the clock was serviced and presented to the National Watch & Clock Museum at Columbia, PA, in 1979, where it remains to this day on prominent display.[17]

Figure 78

Clock 1-E is nearly identical to the case of Clock 1-C; it has the same turned columns with some original and some restored stenciling.

The column turnings on *Clock 1-E* carry over from *Clocks 1-C and 1-D*, and the dial has the same general layout as those clocks as well. Just as with *Clock 1-C*, this case has flat sides and a flat front on the lower cabinet drawer. Original glass drawer pulls are found on this clock.

Most notably, the movement of *Clock 1-E* is stamped with the number "**6**" and the year "**1832**" on the right front of the back plate between the great wheel and the upper right plate pillar post. A view of the movement and stamped numbers is shown in **Figure 79**. Also note that on the opposite side of the back plate is the stamped number "**3**," as yet unexplained.

The dial hands on this clock (*see Figure 80*) are the same as on *Clocks 1-C and 1-D*, establishing this as the most common hand pattern found on early Abner Jones shelf clocks.

As with *Clock 1-C*, this case appears with the weight pulleys incorporated into the wooden top board of the case. Owing to all of the similarities, one could pragmatically assert that the cases of *Clock 1-C and 1-E* were made at the same time.

———— *Figure 79* ————

Front view of the back plate of the movement from Clock 1-E, showing the number "6" and date "1832" on the right side of the plate, and the number "3" on the opposite side.

Photo Courtesy Evan Edwards

———— *Figure 80* ————

Dial close-up of Clock 1-E showing the cut-steel hand pattern most commonly found on early Abner Jones shelf clocks.

Photo Courtesy Evan Edwards

Lastly, just like *Clock 1-D*, the inside of this case is lined with wallpaper. A close-up of this pattern is shown in **Figure 82**. With one known exception, this is the only original wallpaper design found in Abner Jones' shelf clocks to date.

Clocks 1-F through 1-I

Having established the parameters and characteristics of the **Group One** clocks with our first five examples, we will review through pictures and text the remaining survivors found to date. *Clock I-F* is shown in **Figure 81**.

The clock hands are the now-familiar "standard" pattern and the center dial is also painted gold, an attractive touch.

With respect to the main dial, however, this clock deviates from the pattern found on *Clocks 1-C through E*, in that the chapter ring is now approximately 1¼" wide and the wider ring better fills the void between it and the decorated spandrels.

The original drawer pulls have been replaced on this case. Like *Clocks 1-D and 1-E*, the inside of this case is lined with wallpaper, and a view of this paper is shown in **Figure 82**.

The movement in *Clock 1-F* is not numbered. This clock was once owned by the late Doug Blazey of Victor, NY, a wonderful gentleman, an astute collector and an early devotee of Abner Jones (and many other upstate New York makers). Doug was the person who originally encouraged Evan Edwards to research this maker.

Chapter Three • 45

Figure 81

The case of Clock 1-F is essentially identical to that of Clock 1-D, with rounded sides, a round base cabinet drawer and internal weight pulleys, but with gold-painted columns which may originally have been gilt.

Photo Courtesy Cottone's Auctions

Figure 82

On several Group One clocks the inside back boards are lined with wallpaper. All are of the same pattern, shown here from Clock 1-F.

The last four **Group One** clocks known to the author are detailed below. All are similar in many respects to the clocks we have previously examined. Only one has wallpaper on the inside of the case; all have internal weight pulleys, and one of the four has flat sides and a flat lower cabinet drawer front.

On each of the previous **Group One** time-and-strike movement clocks shown, the bell was installed above the movement, mounted horizontally, screwed into the bottom of the top board. One somewhat odd development shared by all four of our remaining clocks is that each utilizes a bell cast too large to fit on the top board and still allow the case door to close.

This curious decision, apparently deliberate, had consequences. In order to fit in the cases, the larger bells were screwed into the back board and mounted vertically above the movement. To provide clearance, a hole was literally cut/gouged into the top board of each of these clocks so that the bell would fit, as shown in *Figure 83*. Visually, the result, with a portion of the bell sticking out above the top board, is rather ungainly. Perhaps Jones got complaints that the bell sound was too soft enclosed within the case. The approximately 1" thick top board would limit sound transfer. While most of these large clocks would have been mounted on mantels at such a height that only an extremely tall individual would ever be able see the protrusion, the act is a bit of an offense to the aesthetic. As we will see, many later clocks continued this arrangement, which supports the idea that this was a deliberate move.

Figure 83

In several Group One clocks, bells cast too large to fit otherwise are mounted vertically above the movement, and protrude through a hole cut into the top board.

Chapter Three • 47

Figure 84
Clock 1-G, owned by the Granger Homestead, Canandaigua, NY.

Figure 85

Clock I-H *showing a new turning pattern on the columns and possibly modified dial and hands.*

Chapter Three • 49

Clock 1-G is shown in **Figure 84**. It is owned by and exhibited in the Granger Homestead, a nonprofit historical institution housed in a wonderful Federal mansion at Canandaigua, NY.

This case has flat sides and a flat front lower cabinet drawer. The drawer pulls are original. The turned column form agrees with *Clocks 1-C through 1-F* with stenciling – likely restored in the author's opinion – over stained wood. This clock has wallpaper lining the back board and has internal weight pulleys.

The movement in this clock is not numbered. This clock contains a repainted dial and brass hands. The hour hand has an open heart-shaped form and the minute hand a bulbous pointer, both standard on later Jones clocks. These hands will be discussed in **Chapter Four**, but the hands on this clock are clearly new replacements. The dial format, numerals and spandrel decorations are also typical of *later* Abner Jones clocks.

It is well established that some of the **Group One** clocks have lost their original cut-steel hands over the years for the styled brass hands used on later Abner Jones clocks. The latter were thought to be more "correct" because they were more commonly seen. It is also possible that when an individual dial needed restoration the owner had it repainted in the later, more recognized and accepted format as seen here. Not to be lost, however, is the fact that all of the **Group Two** clocks that we will review next have the "new" hands and revised dials, and we don't absolutely know when those transitions took place.

Clock 1-H is shown in **Figure 85**. This case has rounded sides and a lower cabinet drawer with a rounded front. The drawer pulls are original.

This clock has internal weight pulleys and the movement is not numbered.

This clock has a new *turned column format*, with the lower half similar to previous models, but with four rope turnings in the middle and a series of bulbous turnings at the top. The stenciling on the columns is original with some touch-ups. The inside of the case is *not* lined with wallpaper.

The bell protrusion on this clock is covered by a wooden "box" to keep dust out of the case.

The inner dial features a seconds bit with a nice, original pointer hand (*see Figure 86*).

Unlike any other **Group One** Abner Jones shelf clock with an otherwise original dial, this dial features Roman numerals. With all other aspects of the dial format being similar to *Clock 1-F*, and with the hand-drawn quality of these numerals, it would appear likely that this is an original dial with a repainted and renumbered chapter ring.

Figure 86

Close-up of the inner dial seconds bit of Clock 1-H *showing the original pointer hand.*

Our next example, *Clock 1-I*, is shown in **Figure 87**. This clock is in the collection of the Hoffman Clock Museum at Newark, NY. The museum is supported by an endowment from Augustus and Jennie Hoffman, who donated their extensive clock collection to be housed in a wing of the Newark Public Library. The museum has a general offering but places an emphasis on New York State clocks.

This case has rounded sides and a rounded-front lower cabinet drawer. The drawer has replaced wood pulls. The case has internal weight pulleys and does not have wallpaper in the interior.

The column turning pattern is *nearly* a duplicate of those found on *Clock 1-H*, but this design has *five* rope turnings instead of the four on the previous clock. The bell does protrude from the top board but not nearly so much as in *Clock 1-H*.

The inner and outer dials have clearly been repainted, with seemingly improper Roman numerals, so it cannot be determined if this clock once had a dial format similar to the others in this Group. In addition, the hands are the "later" Jones brass style, with the same caveat.

One very interesting feature, first appearing in this clock and also several other later Jones clocks, is what Evan Edwards described as a "planetary winding arrangement" or, in English parlance, "Epicyclic Maintaining Power" on the time side great wheel. The extra internal gearing on the

Figure 87

Clock 1-I *owned by the Hoffman Clock Museum, Newark, NY.*

Chapter Three • 51

time side great wheel makes it substantially easier to wind the weight up, but at the cost of three times as many cranks. The gearing retains around three-fourths of the normal driving torque on the gear train under winding, thus it is a form of maintaining power.[18] Pictures of this movement feature are shown in **Figures 88 and 89**.

Figures 88 & 89

Time side great wheel of the Hoffman Museum clock showing the addition of the planetary winding gear that makes it easier to wind the clock.

Photos Courtesy Evan Edwards

And Now for Something Different!

Last (for now, as there are almost certainly more **Group One** examples out there waiting to be uncovered) but not least is our example *Clock 1-J*. As the reader will have deduced by now, the Abner Jones study is part forensics, part guesswork, and our last clock in **Group One** demands both. This is a clock that the author originally had only seen in a photo shown in an advertisement for the now-defunct Page Auction firm of Batavia, NY. The event was an auction of the estate of Clayton Smith held on June 9, 1999. The clock pictured was intriguing then and remains so now.

The 1999 auction ad is pictured in *Figure 90*. An Abner Jones clock, designated *Clock 1-J* is featured at the bottom of the page – an early case variation never before seen. An enlargement of the clock in the ad is shown in *Figure 91*.

The case has several curious aspects. The most obvious is, of course, that the cabinet base has only a single full drawer with a rounded front, unique among the **Group One** clocks. As we will see, some later clocks do have this single-drawer feature.

Figure 90

Page Auctioneers & Appraisers, Batavia, NY, ad for the "Clayton Smith Estate Clock Collection Auction."

GALLERY LOCATION – 5596 EAST MAIN STREET ROAD
BATAVIA, NEW YORK 14020
(716) 343-2934 • (800) PAGE-540

Clayton Smith Estate
Clock Collection Auction

**SATURDAY, JUNE 9
10:00 A.M.**

Preview Times
Friday, June 8
1:00 P.M. to
5:00 P.M.

Saturday, June 9
8:30 A.M. to
10:00 A.M.

< Attrib. Abner Jones, E. Bloomfield, NY, 8-Day Empire Shelf Clock

Source: Page Auctions.

Figure 91

Enlargement of the photo of Clock 1-J, *showing* Group One *features, but with only a single drawer within a shortened cabinet section. The top has a cover to hide the bell protrusion.*

Figure 92

A contemporary view of Clock 1-J *with restored dials.*

Similar to several of the other **Group One** clocks, the bell on *Clock 1-J* protrudes through the top board and is covered by a wooden box. The auction photo shows a dial with a seconds bit, later brass hands and an obviously repainted main dial.

The column turnings do not exactly match any of the other **Group One** cases we have seen, but are certainly typical of and similar to other examples, especially *Clocks 1-H and 1-I*.

Efforts by the author to find and examine this clock continued, with the hope that in time perhaps it would reemerge for study and verification.

Hope won out when the same clock, seemingly well maintained and with an amateur approximation of the painted dials (with Roman instead of the likely proper Arabic numerals), appeared in a summer, 2020 upstate New York auction. A photo of this now-documented clock as restored by its new owner is shown in **Figure 92**.

Conclusions: A New Enterprise — 1828-33

By 1831-32, Abner Jones had successfully transitioned from a brass founder and tall clockmaker, to a brass founder and farmer, to a brass founder, farmer and shelf clockmaker. From the extant **Group One** clocks, his offerings were unique expressions of precision timepieces in high-Empire furniture form. The evolution of the **Group One** clocks shows an energy for and interest in aesthetic improvements that would appear to reflect and result from market acceptance. It would be helpful to know what Abner's annual clock production might have been, but we lack enough numbered and dated movements to come up with much specificity. It appears clear that the **Group One** clocks and, in all likelihood, most if not all of the **Group Two** clocks detailed below, were produced between 1831 and 1835 at the town of Bloomfield (after 1833 the *town of East Bloomfield*) property.[19]

For a detailed comparison of all of the Group One clocks, see Appendix A.

[1] Manke, Robert. *Genealogy of Abner Jones of Pittsfield* (unpublished manuscript, November 2018).

[2] *1830 U.S. Census* for Bloomfield, NY.

[3] Manke.

[4] Walling, H.F. *1852 Map of Ontario County, New York*, Philadelphia, PA, 1852.

[5] *1840 U.S. Census* for East Bloomfield, NY.

[6] Ontario County Deeds Book 52, p. 355 and Mortgages Book 17, p. 332.

[7] Ontario County Mortgage Book 17, p. 465.

[8] Ontario County Mortgage Book 17, p. 333.

[9] Beers, D.G. *Map of Ontario County, New York, 1859*. A.R.Z. Dawson Publishing Co., Philadelphia, PA, 1859.

[10] Google Earth, East Bloomfield, NY, 2020.

[11] Wikipedia.org. *Greek Revival Period; Empire Furniture*.

[12] Roberts, Kenneth and Taylor, Snowden. *Eli Terry and the Connecticut Shelf Clock*, and *Connecticut Clock Technology 1810-1862: The Contributions of Joseph Ives*, Kenneth Robert Publishing, Fitzwilliam, NH. 1973; 1988.

[13] Oechsle, G. Russell and Boyce, Helen. *An Empire In Time: Clocks & Clock Makers of Upstate New York*. National Association of Watch & Clock Collectors, Inc., Columbia, PA, 2003, pp. 93-97.

[14] Ibid.

[15] Correspondence with Marilyn Fitch, October, 2004; June, 2005.

[16] Correspondence with Tom Grimshaw, October, 2019; March, 2020.

[17] Correspondence with Pat Tally, Town of West Bloomfield, NY, historian and descendent of the Baker and White families, May, 2020.

[18] Edwards, Evan. *Abner Jones Clockmaker* (unpublished manuscript, August 1982).

[19] French, J.H. *Gazetteer of the State of New York*, Syracuse, NY, R. Pearsall Smith, Pub., 1860, p. 496.

CHAPTER FOUR
Shelf Clock Transitions – 1833-35

Group Two – Things Change and Standardize

The next iteration of Abner Jones' shelf clocks is detailed here as "**Group Two**." **Group Two** clocks are slightly revised variations of the Group One cases, and exhibit more uniformity than their predecessors. A typical Group Two example, designated *Clock 2-A*, is shown in **Figure 93**.

Figure 93

Clock 2-A - *Typical case configuration of the Group Two clocks.*

Chapter Four • 55

The Case of Clock 2-A

The case is pine with solid and veneer mahogany. **The height of the case is approx. 41".** *Overall heights can vary among* **Group Two** *examples due to differences in the height of the carved paw feet.* **Width at the cabinet base is 17⅞", width of the central case is 15" and width of the top cornice board is 19¾". Depth at the base is 7½", at the central case 6½", and depth of the top board is 9".** *The dimensions of the cases in* **Group Two** *are more consistent than those in* **Group One***, but these were still handmade, and individual dimensions do vary by up to 1".*

Group Two cases are clearly derivative of the earlier cases, but more uniform. *All of these cases have* **three drawers**. As with **Group One**, *all have paw feet*, some more delicate than others. The delicate ones seem almost too insubstantial to support the large upper case. *All of the case sides are now* **flat**. *Most of the cases have lower cabinet drawers with flat fronts.* *All of the observable clocks have* **wallpaper lining** *the inside of the cases.* Original drawer pulls still appear to have been white glass.

The fundamental case modification found with the **Group Two** clocks involves the cornice tops, which carry the addition of an approximately 2" high "box" section between the central case and the cornice top board. A comparison of the **Group One and Two** case tops showing the new component is shown in **Figure 94**.

This results in a taller case, and with the **Group Two** cases measuring approximately 2" less in width at the top board, and measuring around ¾" less in width at the base, they are leaner than the **Group One** cases as well. The result is more a more imposing and certainly attractive case, but changing the design of an apparently successful case involves a rational decision. Why add the box? The most obvious reason, if correct, harkens back to the bell placements appearing on several of the late **Group One** clocks. The new tops solve the situation of the unattractive bell protrusions by neatly providing a cover. With the new upper "surround," *all of the extant Group Two clocks have* **weight pulleys built into the top board**.

Starting with the **Group Two** clocks, the rounded side treatment seen on many of the Group One cases disappears permanently, but both flat front and rounded front lower cabinet drawers continue to be used.

The turned columns on all of the Group Two clocks are the same, as shown in **Figure 95**. The column shown retains original stenciling and gilt paint. Most of the other **Group Two** clocks share these features, some repainted, some without stenciling, and one survives with stained wood columns.

Clock 2-A and several other of the seven **Group Two** cases documented to date by this author have trim edge mahogany molding around each of the cabinet drawers, an attractive embellishment.

Figure 94

Comparison of the Case Top Construction of Abner Jones' Group One *(top) and* Group Two *(bottom) shelf clocks.*

Figure 95

Standard turned columns found on the Group Two clocks.

Figure 96

Typical dial found on extant, original, clocks in Group Two, with stylized Arabic numerals and green, gold and red decorated spandrels.

The Dial

Another major change made to the new series of cases involves the clock dials. The center/inner dial remains, and the outer dial still attaches to the door, but the dial opening on the **Group Two** grows slightly from 9½" square with **Group One**, to 9¾" square. On the **Group Two** clocks, the main dial chapter ring and the spandrels receive a totally revised format. Arabic numerals are retained on all of the extant original dials in this group, but they are much larger within a chapter ring now measuring approximately 1¾" wide. All of the extant original dials in this group have similar decorative spandrels. The typical **Group Two** dial format and decorative treatment is shown in *Figure 96*.

As previously noted, the zinc dial plates had obvious drawbacks as paintable surfaces. While an issue on several of the **Group One** dials, that group of clocks actually fared well as compared with the obvious deterioration of the painted dials on many of Abner Jones' later clocks. An example of what many owners have confronted is shown in *Figure 97*. Fortunately, a number of talented dial restorers have been available over the years to either repaint these dials with exact appropriate details or to touch up deteriorated areas while retaining what they could of original portions. As such, it remains a basic fact that finding an Abner Jones shelf clock with an excellent original dial can be very difficult.

Chapter Four • 57

Figure 97

A typical Abner Jones delaminated dial.

Figure 98

Typical dial and spandrel detail found on known original Group Two clocks.

A close-up of the decorated spandrels found on a typical **Group Two** dial is shown in **Figure 98**. The decorative painting on all of Abner Jones' dials can reasonably be called simplistic and perhaps even described as folk art.

Clock 2-A is one of the two Abner Jones clocks in the collection of the East Bloomfield, NY, Historical Society. The clock was donated by Margaret Elle, descendant of an East Bloomfield family.

The case appears to be largely original with the exception of the added stencil decorations on the turned columns.

The New Hands

One of the distinguishing features of Abner Jones' shelf clocks are his distinctive cast brass hands. Over the years, it has generally been held that all Abner Jones shelf clocks had these hands. New evidence supports the fact that this was not the case, and that while these "typical" hands were not used on the earliest Jones shelf clocks, they were adopted soon thereafter and retained for the duration of shelf clock production. It simply cannot be determined whether any of the **Group One** clocks originally had brass hands, but we can clearly say that by the time **Group Two** production started, the switch had been made. As this is such a notable component of the Jones shelf clocks, some characteristics will be reviewed.

Figure 99 shows a **Group Two** dial with the new hand style. As we know, both hands on Jones' shelf clocks are the same length, so a novel design was required to offer a visual differentiation. This is accomplished quite successfully

Figure 99

Examples of the "standard" solid brass hands found on most Abner Jones shelf clocks. Note the tiny screw at the base of the hour hand that secures the hand to the hour pipe.

with the new cast brass hands by utilizing a large, open-heart shape at the end of the hour hand and a smaller, solid spade end on the minute hand.

Another in a long line of unusual features on Abner Jones' shelf clocks is his method of securing the hour hand to the hour pipe. Rather than employing a friction fit or using a conical collar to the secure the hand as on many other clocks, Jones went to considerable trouble to drill and thread a hole in the base edge of the hour hand to accommodate a tiny screw. This example of Abner Jones' emphasis on quality and craftsmanship over production efficiencies can actually be useful in determining the originality of some restorations. Drilling and threading the brass hand collar to accommodate a tiny screw is not something that many restorers will take the time to replicate, so in most cases (there are certainly exceptions), beautiful cast brass hands that look exactly like originals but lack the screw arrangement can be considered likely non-original.

The interior of the case showing the wallpaper lining found on all known examples of **Group Two** clocks is shown in *Figure 100*. This is the same wallpaper found in several of the Group One clocks.

Clock 2-B is shown in **Figure 101**. It retains nearly all of its original features with the exception of the replaced drawer pulls and repairs to portions of the dial. Note that the lower drawer is rounded on this case.

Clock 2-B reconnects us with the ongoing issue of the numbers found on only some of the extant Jones shelf clocks. When last we left **Group One**, the highest number recorded on a clock was "6."

Figure 101
Clock 2-B *displaying many of the original features found on the* Group Two *clocks.*

Figure 100
Interior detail of Clock 2-A *showing the wallpaper lining found on all of the* Group Two *clocks.*

Figures 102A & B
This apparent number "4" stamping is found on the movement of Clock 2-B.

The movement of *Clock 2-B* is stamped with what appears to be the number "4" (*see Figures 102A and B*). *This is the only Group Two clock found to date with a numbered movement.*

Now, it may well be the number "4." The **Group One and Two** clocks certainly appear to have been made contemporaneously, and there is no reason why movement "4" could not have been pulled off the shelf, so to speak, for placement in this case. The confusing factor, however, is that this stamping appears in a variety of ways on later clocks, both as numbers and seemingly as an extraneous symbol of some sort.

One interesting feature of the stamping design is that if it is turned upside down, it becomes the number "7," and it is used as such on several Jones movements.

Photos of the additional **Group Two** clocks known by the author or recorded by Evan Edwards are shown in **Figures 103-107**.

Clock 2-C (*see Figure 103*) is an excellent example overall, with original stenciled columns and drawer pulls with a flat front lower drawer like *Clock 2-A*. The dial has been restored with likely inappropriate Roman numerals. All of the other known **Group Two** clocks with original dials have Arabic numerals.

Clock 2-D (*see Figure 104*) presents attractively and differs from the other extant **Group Two** clocks in that the turned columns are stained wood. The lower drawer front is round, the drawer pulls are wood and the dial restored.

Clock 2-E (*see Figure 105*) is largely intact, with black and gilt paint on the columns but no stenciling. It has a flat front lower drawer like *Clocks 2-A and 2-C*, original drawer pulls, and a repainted dial. This is a clock inventoried by Evan Edwards but not located or seen by the author.

Clock 2-F (*see Figure 106*) has an original dial showing the typical delamination of paint, a round front lower drawer with replaced drawer pulls and repainted or retouched black and gilt columns without stenciling. The feet are missing. This clock, once owned by collector Bryson Moore, was donated to and now resides at the National Watch & Clock Museum at Columbia, PA.

Clock 2-G (*see Figure 107*) is a fine example; largely original with a flat lower drawer and original stenciling on the columns. The drawer pulls are wood and the dial has been restored.

The **Group One and Two** Abner Jones shelf clocks represent a family unto themselves. Later examples show clear departures from these earlier case and dial styles. The subsequent phases of Jones' case development likely went hand-in-hand with his sale of the homestead, foundry and farm property in East Bloomfield in May, 1835.

On May 1, 1835, Abner and Sabra sold all of their properties in the town of East Bloomfield, including Lots #62 and #77, to Alonson Parmele (predecessor to G.N. Parmele as shown on the 1852 Map in **Figure 39**) for a sale price of $4,400, subject to the unpaid $1,500 portion of the mortgage held by Evan Johns (*Ontario County, NY, Deeds, Book 57, p. 429*). The family was on the move again.

Considering the apparent production period at the town of East Bloomfield property running from 1831 to the sale of that property in early 1835, the author feels it is fair to presume that all of the **Group One and Two** clocks were produced at that location. How the introduction of new case designs coincided with the move to a new base of operations will be discussed in **Chapter Five**.

For a detailed comparison of all of the Group Two clocks, see Appendix B.

Figure 103
Clock 2-C

Figure 104
Clock 2-D

Photo Courtesy Cottone's Auctions

Chapter Four • 61

Figure 105
Clock 2-E

Figure 106
Clock 2-F

Photo Courtesy Evan Edwards –
Archives of the American Clock & Watch Museum

Photo Courtesy Evan Edwards –
Archives of the American Clock & Watch Museum

Figure 107
Clock 2-G

Photo Courtesy John Fadden

CHAPTER FIVE

1835 – Clock Making Begins at West Bloomfield

With the sale of the town of East Bloomfield homestead, farm, foundry and clock shop on May 1, 1835, Abner and Sabra Jones moved with their family approximately six miles west to the settlement and (new) town of West Bloomfield, reflecting the subdivision of the town of Bloomfield into East and West portions in 1833.

As noted, the East Bloomfield propery was sold to Alonson Parmele for $4,400, subject to the $1,500 mortgage held by Evan Johns given to him by Abner and Sabra on March 31, 1832. It is unclear if this lien was actually repaid at the time of the sale of the farm, as the mortgage was not officially discharged by Johns until April 2, 1840.[1] It is possible that Johns allowed the Joneses to carry the obligation forward to give Abner more capital with which to establish his new clock operation.

On July 1, 1835, Abner and Sabra completed the purchase, for $2,000, of a house and 28-acre farm lot on the north side of the State Road in West Bloomfield from owner Charles Webb. The property was about ¼ mile west of the four corners at the center of the village.[2] Despite the fact that they had, on paper, earned a profit of at least $2,900 from the sale of the East Bloomfield property, the Joneses signed a mortgage of $1,700 over to Webb at the time of the purchase, perhaps in order to cover the capital expenses of starting operations in their new location.[3]

No circa 1835 maps of West Bloomfield exist, but the location of the Abner Jones property can be identified using the 1852 and 1859 Ontario County Maps.[4]

Figure 108 shows the 1852 map of the town. The area outlined is detailed in *Figures 109 and 110*.

―――――― *Figure 108* ――――――

1852 Map of the town of West Bloomfield, NY. The area outlined is detailed in Figure 109.
(Walling, H.F 1852 Map of Ontario County, New York.)

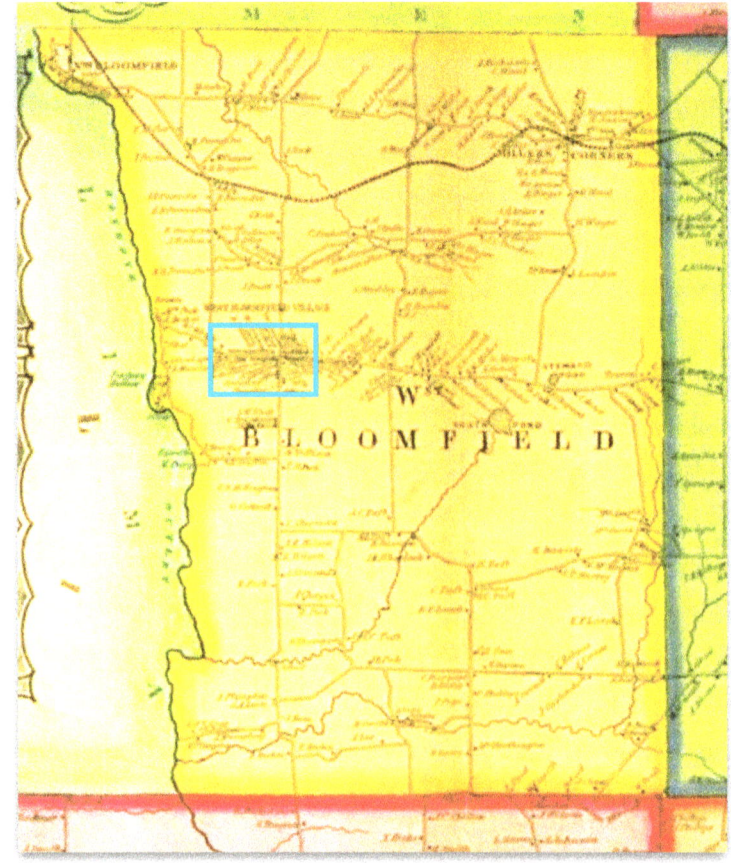

Figure 109 shows a close-up view of the village of West Bloomfield circa 1859. The Abner Jones house, farm and clock shop lot is outlined. In 1859 it was owned by James H. Hall.[5]

Figure 110 shows the insert in greater detail. As of 1859, the Jones property was owned by James H. Hall, with Hall's house situated on the west side of the lot and his brewery, carriage factory and blacksmith shop to the east.

Figure 109

Detail of the Village of West Bloomfield from D.G. Beers' 1859 Map of Ontario County, NY. The location of the Abner Jones property purchased in 1835 on the north side of the State Road (now U.S. Route 20 and NY Route 5) is partially outlined.

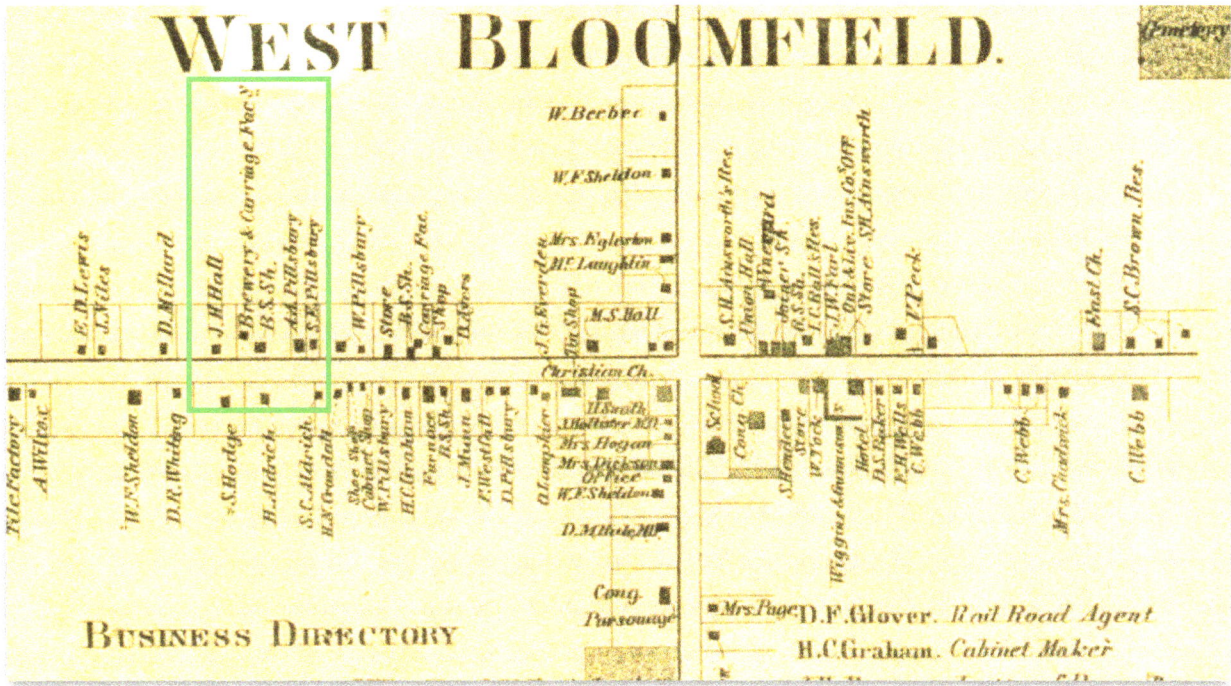

Figure 110

A reoriented portion of the 1859 map of the village of West Bloomfield showing the location of the Abner Jones property as it then existed.

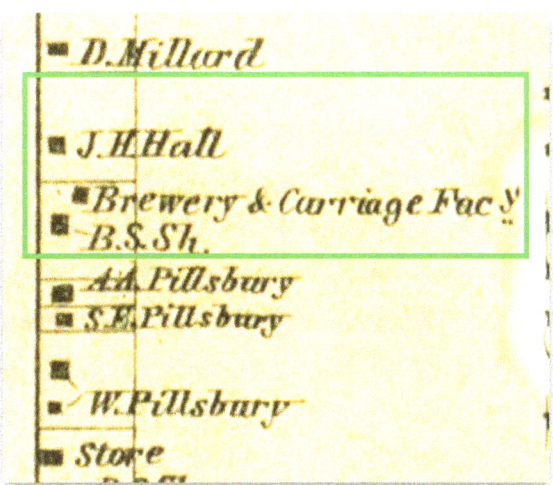

The buildings that currently exist on the circa 1835 Abner Jones property at West Bloomfield are shown in **Figures 111 and 112**. The underlying basic architecture of the home appears to be of the 1830 period, and may be the actual Jones homestead, but with many alterations. The commercial building on the site has clearly been modified over the years and is difficult to date.

Figure 111

This home on the site of the Abner and Sabra Jones residence at West Bloomfield may be their original residence.

Figure 112

This commercial and residential building currently sits on the site of Abner Jones' foundry and clock making operations at West Bloomfield. The Turnpike (U.S. 20 & NY 5) is in the foreground.

Clock Making in Context – Measuring Up Abner Jones' Upstate New York Competition in 1835

As previously noted, when Abner Jones entered the upstate New York "niche" market for large, stylish, expensive 8-day brass movement clocks around 1831, his primary competitor was Asa Munger of Auburn, NY. As this market segment remained strong into the mid-1830s, other upstate New York entrants emerged to compete with Munger and Jones. The first was **Jared Arnold, Jr.**, a transplant from Connecticut with apparent firsthand experience in making Bristol, CT, inventor Joseph Ives' new 8-day "strap-brass" roller pinion movements that used less brass and were thus cheaper to make than other brass movement clocks on the market. Movements of Ives' design were produced and marketed by the Bristol, CT, firm of C. & L.C. Ives, and by the firms of John Birge, who placed them in attractive "triple-decker" cases designed by Elias Ingraham of Bristol, CT.[6]

Arnold arrived at the tiny hamlet of Amber, Onondaga County, NY, on the shore of Otisco Lake, one of the smallest of the Finger Lakes, in late 1832 and immediately began making "triple-decker" clocks with his own variation of the Ives strap, roller pinion movement. An example of one of Arnold's clocks is shown in **Figure 113**, and one of his two unique 8-day movements is pictured in **Figure 114**.

Arnold was a steady producer of these attractive clocks until early 1838 when he ceased production due to the nationwide economic crisis that began in 1837.[7]

Working with Arnold was **Philip Smith**, an Amber resident who had been making clock cases, importing wooden works movements, and selling clocks with his own labels since the late 1820s. After working with Jared Arnold, Jr. for about a year and a half, Smith saw an opportunity and left Amber to move about 10 miles north to the village of Marcellus, Onondaga County, NY, where, by mid-1833, he had established a clock factory on Nine Mile Creek, a veritable Mississippi compared to the source of water power available to Arnold at the Amber, NY, site.

At Marcellus, Smith continued to market cheaper clocks with wooden works movements, but specialized in 8-day brass, weight-driven, Empire-style clocks in several designs, all of them meeting the "large, stylish, expensive" standard. Two of Smith's most common 8-day brass movement case styles are shown in **Figures 115 and 116**, and two of Smith's unique 8-day brass movements (he utilized five at last count…) are pictured in **Figures 117 and 118**.

Figure 113

Triple-decker cased clock with 8-day strap brass movement by Jared Arnold, Jr.

Figure 114

8-day strap brass movement by Jared Arnold, Jr. of Amber, Otisco, NY. These are clearly derivative of the movements invented by Joseph Ives of Bristol, CT, but vary in several unique ways.

Photo Courtesy Jim DuBois

Figure 115
Full column and cornice shelf clock by Philip Smith.

Photo Courtesy Cottone's Auctions

Figure 116
Smith's most common 8-day case style.

Figure 117
One of Smith's 8-day brass movements, this is dubbed the "strap" model.

Photo Courtesy Cottone's Auctions

Figure 118
Another of Smith's 8-day brass movements, this is the "solid plate" model.

Photo Courtesy Cottone's Auctions

Philip Smith remained active at Marcellus before finally succumbing to economic forces and angry creditors in 1842.[8]

In March, 1833, almost certainly in reaction to mounting competition, **Asa Munger** and partner **Thaddeus Benedict**, who had joined him in the clock making enterprise by 1831 as **Munger & Benedict**, made a momentous decision to sign a contract with the State of New York to employ prisoners at the Auburn State Prison to make their clocks. They took on a third partner in **Clarke Beers Hotchkiss**, and the first prison-manufactured clocks bore the firm name "**Asa Munger & Co.**" The move was controversial and it may have affected Munger's primary jewelry and silversmith business, as he officially left the partnership in July, 1834 but appears to have remained a silent partner thereafter in the firm of **Hotchkiss & Benedict**. Hotchkiss & Benedict produced around 3,500 clocks utilizing prison labor before ending the business in 1836. Their clocks lacked nothing in the way of craftsmanship or design despite the use of prison labor. An Asa Munger & Co. clock is shown in in **Figure 119**, and a Hotchkiss & Benedict product in **Figure 120**.[9]

Figure 119
Asa Munger & Co. ca. 1833-34 shelf clock produced at Auburn State Prison.

Figure 120
Typical 8-day shelf clock produced ca. 1834-36 by Hotchkiss & Benedict with prison labor.

By 1830, the village of Seneca Falls, located approximately 15 miles west of Auburn and 40 miles east of West Bloomfield, was a bustling manufacturing center due to its favorable location on the Seneca River flowing north from Seneca Lake, and on the adjacent Cayuga-Seneca Canal, which linked both Seneca and Cayuga Lakes to the Erie Canal to the north.

In 1834, Chauncey Marshall, a local businessman, and Elmer W. Adams, a Connecticut native with experience in the clock industry, partnered to form the firm of **Marshall & Adams**. By late that year they had established their factory on a strip of land with the river (and water power) on one side and the canal on the other and started to produce clocks. As with Philip Smith, they marketed cheaper wood works clocks, but their prime products were 8-day brass movement clocks in a variety of cases. In 1836, Adams bought out Marshall and the firm's name changed to "E.W. Adams," but the product line remained consistent. Two of the most common Marshall & Adams/E.W. Adams 8-day shelf clock case styles are shown in *Figures 121 and 122*.

The most common 8-day brass movement (there were two) used by Marshall & Adams and E.W. Adams is shown in *Figure 123*.

Along with many other manufacturers (clock and otherwise), both Marshall and Adams became victims of the severe nationwide economic downturn that led up to, and then followed, the Panic of 1837. Chauncey Marshall engaged in land speculation and, broken by the economic crash, took his own life on December 31, 1837. Adams was sued in late 1837 by creditors and his shop padlocked by the Sheriff. His remedy was to break

Figure 121

Marshall & Adams full column and cornice shelf clock case: their top-end model.

Figure 122

E.W. Adams carved column and cornice case shelf clock.

Photo Courtesy Cottone's Auctions

into his factory in the dead of night, fill two canal boats with all of his remaining clocks, and escape to Chillicothe, OH, where he spent 1838 selling his inventory.[10]

In light of this competition, the move by Abner Jones to West Bloomfield, coupled with his development of multiple new case designs thereafter, cannot be viewed in a vacuum. In reestablishing himself at West Bloomfield, Jones was making a calculated decision to become a more diversified clockmaker, and this business decision had to be made with his competitors in mind.

Frankly, the odds were not in his favor. From 1834-1836, Hotchkiss & Benedict produced more than 3,500 clocks, and the 8-day brass clocks manufactured by Philip Smith and Marshall & Adams/E.W. Adams likely met or exceeded that number. Jared Arnold, Jr. produced in lesser numbers but certainly many more than the 100 or so theoretically produced over a 10-year period by Jones.[11] So by comparison Jones was, in modern parlance, a "boutique" maker who, by necessity, would have to produce the finest and most attractive product for the most discriminating buyers in order to survive.

As noted, we have no way of knowing exactly where to draw the line between the last East Bloomfield clocks and the first made in 1835 at West Bloomfield, but, as if recognizing our dilemma, two surviving Abner Jones clocks may serve to provide some guidance.

Figure 123

This was the most common 8-day brass movement used in Marshall & Adams and E.W. Adams clocks.

The Clocks of 1835

As luck and circumstances would have it, we are fortunate to find two extant clocks, both with the year "1835" stamped on their movements, to represent the clear transition from the East Bloomfield to the West Bloomfield Abner Jones clocks. These two clocks and others made from between 1835 and 1841 will be grouped by case style. As we will see, unlike the **Groups One and Two** clocks that could realistically be categorized by production date, the clocks made in 1835 and thereafter do not necessarily appear to have been produced in distinct groups, but rather as a variety of styles over time, suggesting, perhaps, that cases could have been made to order.

Our first 1835 clock can be included in what the author has classified as the "**Full Empire Group**," or **Group Three**. None of the cases in this group are exactly alike, but may share features such as the design of specific case elements, column treatment, dial presentation and others. The earliest example of this Group, *Clock 3-A*, is shown in *Figure 124*.

This is a very large case, measuring 49 $\frac{1}{2}$" high with its feet missing, so the full clock, including perhaps another 3" or more for the feet, would come in at **approximately 53" in height, fully a foot taller than the Group Two cases!** *The base cabinet section* is 22 $\frac{5}{8}$" wide, 8 $\frac{1}{2}$" tall and 7" deep. *The main case section* is 36 $\frac{1}{8}$" high, 19 $\frac{3}{4}$" wide and 7" deep, and *the cornice top* is 26 $\frac{1}{8}$" wide, 4 $\frac{1}{2}$" tall and 11" deep.

The dial opening is among the smallest found on any Abner Jones clock, measurning 9 $\frac{5}{8}$" square. This clock's zinc dial, attached to the back of the door as with previous models, features a unique, original, painted motif with *Roman* numerals with a gilt paint decorative trim and simplified gilt outlined corner spandrels otherwise bereft of decoration (**see Figure 125**). The inner dial and hands are attached to the movement in the typical way. *Unique dial sizes and/or treatments are actually typical of this group.* The use of **Roman numerals** on this *and (nearly) all subsequent* Abner Jones clocks is significant, as it represents a clear departure from the **Group One and Two** clocks, and may be one way to clearly distinquish between East and West Bloomfield production and marketing. The change may be a reflection of the intent to increase production volume, as it is demonstrably easier to paint Roman numeral dials than those with Arabic numerals, or it may simply have been based on perceived customer preference.[12]

The secondary wood in the case of *Clock 3-A* is pine under solid and veneer mahogany. The half columns are veneered in tiger maple. The case features four drawers,

Figure 124

Full Empire Group Three Example 3-A, a full-column cornice-top case with four drawers.

Photo Courtesy Evan Edwards

Figure 125

The unique dial treatment found on Clock 3-A, with Roman numerals, which would become the standard for Abner Jones' clocks thereafter, and otherwise austere decorations. The dial measures 9⁷/₈" square, among the smallest of the Jones dials.

Photo Courtesy the Steele Family

Figure 126

The movement of Clock 3-A has one feature not recorded to date on any other Jones clock – an additional arbor on the strike side carrying a pulley designed to keep the weight cord away from the strike side gears and the hammer arbor.

Photo Courtesy the Steele Family

the first appearance of such since its timepiece progenitor. The upper drawers have possibly replaced wood pulls, while the two lower round-front drawers have what appear to be the original bulbous, clear glass pulls.

The clock's original feet were removed, per family lore, when the clock was literally built into a wall at one of the owner's homes at East Bloomfield. *(see the Back Story on page 74)*.

In addition to the remarkable and unusual case, the movement in this clock provides its own surprises. One feature not yet seen on any other Abner Jones movement was the addition of an arbor and pulley on the strike side to facilitate the clearance of the weight cord from the strike side gears and the hammer arbor. A photo of this feature is shown in **Figure 126**.

And other surprises await! A photo of the front of the back plate of the movement of *Clock 3-A* is shown in **Figure 127**, and in more detail in **Figure 128**. As shown, the back of the movement is stamped with the inscription "**1835**"/ "**G.W. Berry**," and the back of the hour gear wheel is also stamped "**W. Berry.**"

This, of course, begs the question "*Who was G. W. Berry?*"

The name on the movement could reasonably, it seems, either represent the original owner of the clock or the name of one of the mechanics who helped make the clock. The latter is not unheard of among early American clock movements. For example, in the wooden works tall clock era, clock assemblers often stamped their initials into the wood seat boards the movements were secured to, giving modern collectors hours of pleasure trying to determine, 200 years later, who "D.S.W." or "T.R." really were.

Members of the Steele family of East Bloomfield, NY, believe that this clock has been with the family since the original sale, and there is no reason to believe otherwise (see the *Back Story* on page 74), leaving the "worker" option the most compelling.[13]

No "G.W. Berry" appears in the *1830 Census* for Bloomfield, NY, but one **Gillman (Gilman) (Ward) Berry** does appear in the *1840 Census for East Bloomfield*, residing there with his wife Roxie (Evarts, whom he married at East Bloomfield in 1836).[14] Further searches indicate that Gilman was born July 16, 1804, the tenth child of William and Rachael (Ward) Berry, at *Pittsfield, NH*, Abner Jones' birthplace.[15] Based on this fact, it appears quite possible that Gillman W. Berry was from a Pittsfield, NH, family known to Abner Jones, and that he was recruited to move to New York to work as a brass caster or finisher/journeyman in Abner's clock factory.

The listings in the *1840 Census* reveal that Berry resided on the same road and within a short distance from Jones' East Bloomfield farm/factory lot. While at East Bloomfield, Berry applied for and was granted a sale of 250 acres of public land in Michigan on May 5, 1837.[16] Sometime after appearing in the *1840 Census* as a New York resident, Berry and his wife moved to this property in Mason, Ingham County, located just south of Lansing, Michigan. Their daughter Alvina died soon after her birth in 1843 at Mason, and their son Ward, born in 1846 at Mason, died at Petersburg, VA on June 19, 1864 as a Private in the Union Army. Gilman himself died September 25, 1872 at Aurelius, Ingham County, MI.[17]

Figures 127 & 128

Figure 127 (Left): Photo of the inside of the back plate of the movement of Clock 3-A *showing the stamped inscriptions "1835" and "G.W.Berry" on the movement and "W. Berry" stamped on the rear if the hour gear.*

Figure 128 (right): Close-up view of the stamped inscriptions found on Clock 3-A.

Photo Courtesy Evan Edwards

Evan Edwards had the opportunity to work on this clock at some point and took a photo, as shown in **Figure 129**, of the "exploded" movement and the myriad of components that went into the production of a typical Abner Jones mechanism.

Figure 129

The movement of Clock 3-A showing all of the parts that went into the creation of an Abner Jones 8-day shelf clock movement.

Photo Courtesy Evan Edwards

And Yet Another New Design

Our second 1835 offering represents a fundamental case design change for Abner Jones. Gone were the drawers and cornice tops. Turned columns were joined by carved versions. This clear and deliberate departure from the established "norm" was likely done to address competitive challenges. This clock group, designated **Group Four – the Carved Scroll Case Group**, also has the *most surviving examples of any of Abner Jones' case styles*, almost certainly reflecting the style's popularity. Based on the number of known surviving clocks and movement numbers found on several of them, production of the **Scroll Case** clocks may have run continuously from this 1835 example fully through the rest of the decade.

What may be the first of the Group Four clocks, designated *Clock 4-A*, is shown in **Figure 130**. Its case **measures 37½" high, 17" wide and 6½" deep**. As with all of the other Jones cases, dimensions do differ a bit from clock to clock. While these cases lack drawers and might be presumed to be less imposing than the **Group One and Two** clocks, this is not really so! Note that the **Group Four** cases, at around 38" tall, are just slightly shorter than the **Group One and Two** versions at 39" and 41", respectively.

Clock 4-A has heavily turned, solid mahogany half columns and a scroll-top splat with arching carved acanthus leaves. The plinths are pine with mahogany veneer and the case's secondary wood is pine under mahogany veneer. Rather than a mirror, the lower panel on this case is of figured mahogany veneer. The glass door pull is appropriate and may be original.

CLOCK 3-A: THE BACK STORY

The likely first owner of Clock 3-A was William Steele (b. 1781 at Bethlehem, Litchfield County, CT), who owned a farm directly across the road from Abner Jones' East Bloomfield, NY, farm/factory property in 1835. This lot and other adjacent properties remain in the Steele family to this day. When William passed away in 1858, the clock was inherited by his son Joseph Stanley Steele (1826-1921). The next owner was Joseph's son James Henry Steele (1864-1942), followed by James' son Stanley Oran Steele, (1892-1950), then Stanley's son Stanley Oran Steele, Jr. (1928-1998), and then finally to the present owner, Jeff Steele of East Bloomfield, NY. As noted above, at one of the family's residences at East Bloomfield, the clock was "built into" a wall, and that may have been the reason the original feet were removed from the clock case.[18]

Figure 130

Clock 4-A - *Perhaps the first of the Group Four* scroll-top *cases.*
No inner dial was ever installed on this clock.

Figure 131

Front plate of the movement from Clock 4-A *showing the lack of holes needed to secure the inner dial pillar posts and the brass hands painted white.*

The dial arrangement on *Clock 4-A* is, in terms of the known Abner Jones examples, *almost* unique in that no center dial was ever installed on this clock. This can be conclusively proven by the fact that no holes were ever drilled in the front plate to accommodate the inner dial pillar posts. This original outer dial has been repainted. The brass hands are painted white (likely as original) to contrast with the brass of the movement.

While the movement in *Clock 4-A* is otherwise standard Jones issue, it garners special interest due to the fact that there is a stamped inscription on the front of the back plate just right of the center that reads the number "**1**" over the name "**R.T. Reynolds**" and just below the name is the date "**1835**." A photo of the movement found in *Clock 4-A* is shown in *Figure 131*, and close-ups of the inscriptions on the front of the back plate are pictured in **Figures 132 and 133**.

And, of course, one must ask "*Who was R.T. Reynolds?*" We got lucky with Mr. Berry but alas, efforts to find Mr. Reynolds in any historical records linked to East or West Bloomfield, or anywhere near the area in the 1830-1850 period, proved fruitless. Nonetheless, speculation need not be curtailed!

We can already make an argument that one of Abner Jones' mechanics, Mr. Gilman W. Berry, saw fit to leave his mark for posterity on one of the clocks from the Jones' shop in 1835. The next logical assumption would seem to be that Mr. Reynolds, yet another shop journeyman, was determined to do the same. Furthermore, as perhaps the first movement he helped work on, he may have decided that it warranted the number "1" above his name. Alternate theories are welcomed but they may require another book.

Chapter Six will summarize the **Group Four – Scroll Top Case** clocks identified to date and the variations found within that group. Those concerned with the passing of **Group Three** can be reassured that we will return to that review in **Chapter Eleven**.

Figure 132

Full photo of the front of the back plate of Clock 4-A.

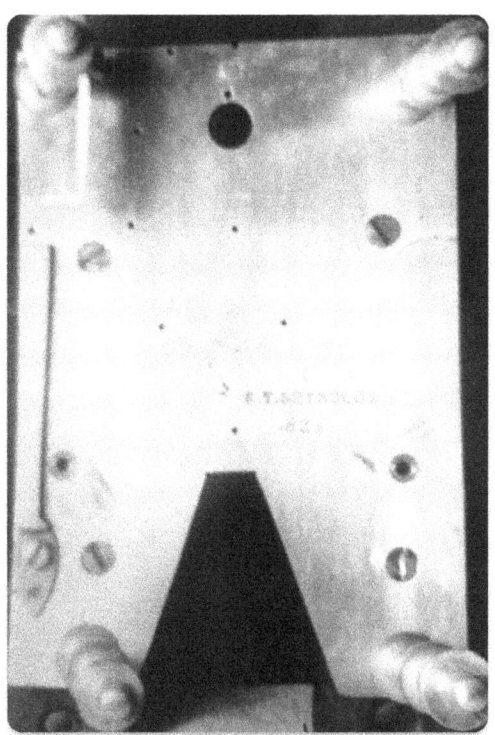

Photo Courtesy Evan Edwards

Figure 133

A close-up view of the inscriptions found on Clock 4-A – "1" / "R.T. Reynolds." / "1835."

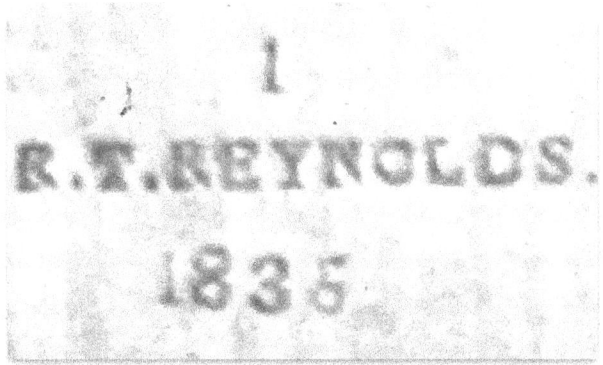

Photo Courtesy Evan Edwards

[1] Ontario County, NY, Mortgages, Book 17, p. 466.

[2] Ontario County, NY, Deeds, Book 58, p. 189.

[3] Ontario County, NY, Mortgages, Book 17, p. 447.

[4] Walling, H.F *1852 Map of Ontario County, New York*.)

[5] Beers, D.G. *1859 Map of Ontario County, NY*.

[6] Roberts, Kenneth and Taylor, Snowden. *Connecticut Clock Technology 1810-1862: The Contributions of Joseph Ives*, Revised Second Edition, Ken Roberts Publishing Co., Fitzwilliam, NH, 1988.

[7] Oechsle, G. Russell and Boyce, Helen. *An Empire In Time: Clocks & Clock Makers of Upstate New York*. National Association of Watch & Clock Collectors, Inc., Columbia, PA, 2003, pp. 3-6.

[8] Ibid. pp. 113-120.

[9] Ibid. pp. 93-97; 63-65.

[10] Ibid. pp. 80-84.

[11] Ibid.

[12] Communication with Lee Davis.

[13] Communication with Jeff Steele.

[14] *1830 and 1840 U.S. Census* for East Bloomfield, NY; marriage research courtesy of Robert Manke.

[15] Ancestry.com. Gilman W. Berry; research courtesy of Robert Manke.

[16] United States Land Patent, Certificate No. 19635, issued to Gilman W. Berry, May 5, 1837, courtesy of Robert Manke.

[17] Ancestry.com. Gilman W. Berry.

[18] Correspondence with Jeff Steele.

CHAPTER SIX

A New Standard

Based on surviving examples, the most common of the new case designs to emerge after Abner Jones' move to West Bloomfield appear to be the **Group Four Carved Scroll Clocks**. They will be examined in this chapter in each of their variations.

The Group Four Clocks

Until this model was introduced, the only carving seen on any Abner Jones cases had been limited to the paw feet. *Clock 4-A* (**see Chapter Five, Figure 130**) seems to have been the prototype for this new design. The turnings on the columns on *Clock 4-A* are complex and the carved scroll splat finely executed. Close-up views of the carved scroll splats found on this and on most of the other **Group Four** clocks are shown in *Figures 134 and 135*. While essentially "identical" there are minor variations in the splats, owing to the fact that each was hand carved. One other distinction is that other than *Clock 4-A*, all of the other identified clocks in **Group Four** appear with brass or wood door pulls, not glass.

Figures 134 & 135

Figures 134 (top) and 135 (bottom):
carved scroll splat detail as found on the Group Four clocks.

78 • *Without Equal: The Clocks of Abner Jones of Bloomfield, New York*

Our first **Group Four subgroup** to be reviewed includes those examples with **Turned Columns, Carved Scroll Splats and Wood Door Panels.** An example is shown in **Figure 136** as *Clock 4-B*. The original dial on this clock features paintings of red flowers and greens in the spandrels (*see Figure 137*). Variations of these painted floral decorations appear on many of the Group Four clocks. The door pull is brass and the door opens with a push-button. The movement in this very original clock is numbered **#49**.

Figures 136 & 137

Figure 136 (left): Clock 4-B with turned columns, carved splat, a wood panel door and an original dial.
Figure 137 (right): The dial of Clock 4-B features a red flower and leaves.

Photo Courtesy Tony Braida

Photo Courtesy Tony Braida

Chapter Six • 79

Another wonderful example of this subgroup is shown in *Figure 138* as *Clock 4-C*. The original dial on this clock features primitively painted shells in the spandrels (*see Figure 139*). The movement in this original clock is numbered **#59**. The door pull is an open brass ring, and the closure is a push-button. *Additional extant clocks in this subgroup are listed in* **Appendix D**.

Figures 138 & 139

Figure 138: (left): Clock 4-C with turned columns, carved splat, a wood panel door and an original dial.

Figure 139: (right): A close-up of the dial of Clock 4-C showing one of the painted shell decorations in the spandrels.

Photo Courtesy Cottone's Auctions

Photo Courtesy Cottone's Auctions

The next **Group Four subgroup** features *Carved Columns, Carved Scroll Splats and Wood Door Panels*. *Figure 140* showcases these elements in *Clock 4-F*. The clock's dial spandrels feature simplified, almost folk art, flowers, similar to but distinct from those seen on *Clock 4-B*. The movement is not numbered. The door pull is brass, and the door has a push-button closure. *Additional extant clocks in this subgroup are listed in* **Appendix D**.

Our **next subgroup** of **Group Four** includes cases with *Turned Columns, Carved Scroll Splats and Mirrors in the Door*.

Clock 4-H, shown in **Figure 141**, includes each of these features. The inner dial of this clock, perhaps a replacement, has a cut-out section in the center through which the front plate of the movement is visible. The door pull is brass and the closure push-button. This clock is from the photo files of Evan Edwards and has not been examined in person by the author. Edwards did not record a movement number.

Figure 140

Clock 4-F *with carved columns, carved splat and wood panel in the door.*

Photo Courtesy Dave Rosen

Figure 141

The turned column, carved splat and mirror door subgroup as represented by Clock 4-H.

Photo Courtesy Evan Edwards

Next, the **Carved Column, Carved Scroll Splat** cases also appear with **Mirrors in the Doors**, as shown by *Clock 4-I* in **Figure 142** below. The movement is not numbered.

To date, only four of the **Group Four Scroll-Top Case Clocks** have been seen with movement numbers. They are *Clocks 4-B (#49) and Clock 4-C (#59) shown above, and Clocks 4-J and 4-K*. The latter two cases have carved columns with mirrors in the door, and they appear with *consecutive numbers, 76 and 77*. The two clocks, with their respective movement numbers, are shown in **Figures 143a-b, and 144a-b,** below. These clocks make productive use of the infamous "7/4" stamp referred to in **Chapter Three**.

Figure 142

Clock 4-I *shows the characteristics of the subgroup with carved column, carved splats and mirrors in the door.*

Photo Courtesy Cottone's Auctions

82 • *Without Equal: The Clocks of Abner Jones of Bloomfield, New York*

Figures 143a & b
Figure 143a (top) Showing Clock 4-J and Figure 143b (bottom) showing the number "76" found on the movement of this clock.

Figures 144a & b
Figure 144a (top) Showing Clock 4-K and Figure 144b (bottom) showing the number "77" found on the movement of this clock.

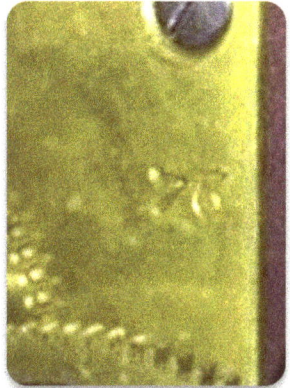

Photos Courtesy Jim Stehlik

Photos Courtesy Frank and Helen Boyce

Chapter Six • 83

An Anomaly on Its Face

By now we have come to expect anomalies from Abner Jones, and **Group Four** offers several, including *Clocks 4-G and 4-N*.

The two clocks differ in their case components. *Clock 4-G*, shown in **Figure 145**, has carved columns, the carved scroll splat and a wood panel door, all features we have seen before, but the columns on this clock have **more intricate and detailed carving than any other Group Four case seen to date.**

Figures 146 and 147 are close-up views of the dial of *Clock 4-G* showing the remnants of what was once a very nice original dial with visions of fruits (apples and pears?) in the spandrels. Last but not least, *Clock 4-G* contains one more anomaly, the method by which its movement is secured in the case. This modification will be reviewed in **Chapter Ten** along with several other movements with this feature.

Clock 4-N, shown in **Figure 148**, is unique among the known **Group Four** clocks in that it has a **Carved Shell Splat and Turned Pad Feet** in addition to its **Turned Columns**, but alas, further information on the clock indicates that the carved splat, and thus likely the entire top, has been replaced.[1] With this otherwise unique feature now eliminated, it appears most likely that this case, too, originally had a carved scroll splat. The level of modification may also put the turned pad feet in doubt, but they do look good!

But what both clocks share in common are **one-piece zinc dials!** These are the only Abner Jones clocks identified to date with this somewhat incongruous feature.

Why incongruous? First, the two-piece dial arrangement is so synonymous with Abner Jones that to find an alternative is a bit shocking. Why mess with a sure (already unique) thing?

Secondly, while most dials found on American shelf clocks in this period were solid and square of both metal and wood, none that the author can recall at the moment, save for several Pennsylvania makers, have full, square dials that nonetheless still *have to be secured by being pinned to the front plate of the movement!* The use, therefore, of a full square dial in this way creates significant logistical problems if one ever has to access the movement.

The pins securing the lower dial pillar posts, positioned at either side of the lower front plate of the movement, are at least nominally accessible by pliers and blind feel. The location of the upper pillar post on the right center of the front plate really requires tiny fingers and a very small pair of pliers and (again) blind feel to reach between the top plate of the case and the top of the dial, not to mention the interference of the mounted bell, to successfully remove the pin securing that post.

This alternate dial design was seemingly not well thought out, perhaps the reason it has been found on a total of only two clocks, both in this **Group Four**, case series.

A further review of *Clock 4-N* in **Figure 148** reveals that this original dial has been improperly repainted with the name of our Abner's third cousin Abner Jones of Weare, NH.

This case has no door pull and a hook-and-eye closure. The interior of this case is covered with two mismatched sections of wallpaper, likely not original.

Figure 149 is a close-up of the incorrectly attributed, repainted dial ("A. Jones/ 1780/ Weare, N.H."), and **Figure 150** shows the back of the original dial with its pillar posts and a view of the interior and movement.

Pictures of this clock were obtained from the Evan Edwards collection and from researcher Terry Brotherton of Texas. It has not been examined by the author, and current ownership is not known. When last seen, it was part of a Texas collection and the clock did appear in the 1999 NAWCC National Convention display at Houston, TX.

For a detailed comparison of all of the Group Four clocks, see Appendix D.

---

[1] 1999 NAWCC National Convention Commemorative Exhibit Catalogue. *Horological Rarities of Space City '99*, p. 6.

Figure 145

Clock 4-G has several notable variations, including more intricately carved columns than others in this Group, and a one-piece dial.

Figures 146 & 147

*Figure 146 (top): Close-up view of the one-piece dial found in Clock 4-G.
As with many Abner Jones dials, the original paint is delaminating from the zinc dial pan.
Figure 147 (bottom): The folk-art images of fruit painted in the spandrels of Clock 4-G.*

86 • *Without Equal: The Clocks of Abner Jones of Bloomfield, New York*

Figure 148

Clock 4-N is only the second Abner Jones shelf clock found with a one-piece dial.
The top capitals and carved shell splat are replacements, and the dial has been incorrectly repainted.

Photo Courtesy Terry Brotherton

Figure 149

The original, but incorrectly repainted, one-piece dial of Clock 4-N that reads "Abner Jones/ 1780/Weare, N.H."

Photo Courtesy Evan Edwards

Figure 150

The back of the one-piece dial, the movement and part of the interior of Clock 4-N.

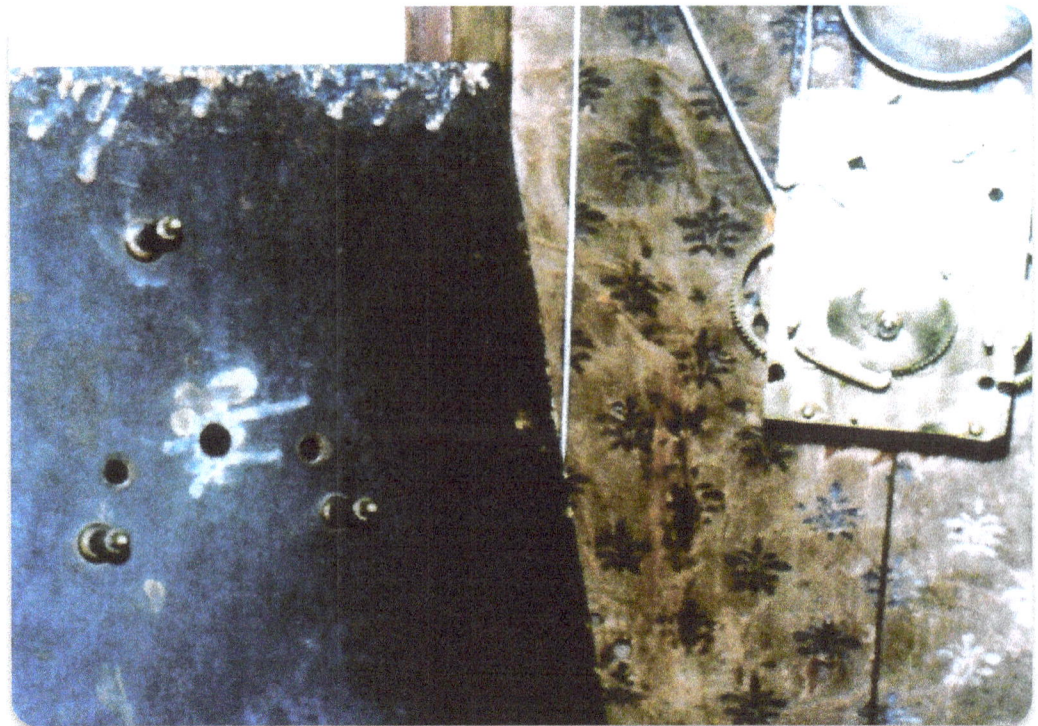

Photo Courtesy Evan Edwards

CHAPTER SEVEN

Who Made the Shelf Clock Cases?

As we know, Abner Jones shelf clocks are synonymous with the big, flamboyant Empire style, and most of the case designs are so unique as to be immediately identifiable at first sight. As we ponder the remarkable case styles already encountered (and with more to come), it appears timely to interject into the Abner Jones story the basic question so many collectors and researchers have had for so long: *"Who made the cases?"*

It would be fair to conclude that Abner Jones, our trained brass founder and clockmaker, did not make his clock cases but procured them from a local cabinetmaker. Just as clear is the fact that he must have had a hand in their design and appearance. Whoever made the cases had to be a talented, clever, experienced cabinetmaker with a wonderful imagination.

As we have seen, the clock cases went through transitions in style and accoutrements as market preferences changed, ranging from the early cases with drawers, paw feet and turned columns to later, smaller (only by Abner Jones standards) models with carved columns and carved scroll splats and no feet, interspersed with multiple "some or all of the above" variations seemingly reflecting the individual preference of the prospective buyer.

Only one extant Abner Jones tall clock contains any reference to a casemaker. As noted in **Chapter Two**, one tall clock has a notation written on the inside of the door stating *"Dec. 1820/ Made by Abner Jones/ Case made by Daniel Miles."* Miles did not appear in the *1820 Census* for Bloomfield, NY, but was described as a resident in several property purchases in East Bloomfield in 1823. In March of that year he bought a house lot in the village *right next to the Jones property*, but owned it for only a month before selling it and buying a commercial establishment on the Village Green called the "Farmer's Store." This would seemingly establish Miles as a general store owner/operator at that point. Miles did not appear in the *1830 Census*, but he was apparently still in East Bloomfield until 1836 when he sold the store to William Prindle and Isaac Mitchell. When that deed was signed, Miles was listed as a resident of York, Livingston County, located approximately 25 miles west of East Bloomfield.[1]

No records found to date provide a clue as to the name of the Jones *shelf clock* casemaker; no ink, pencil or chalk inscriptions on or in the cases, and no extant written histories. But there is one prospective candidate who does stand out: one with a substantial cabinetmaking background who was firmly established at East Bloomfield by 1813. His name is **Simeon Deming**.

Simeon Deming (b. 1769 at Wethersfield, CT, d. 1855 at East Bloomfield, NY) was the son of James Deming of Wethersfield, CT, both members of a long and famous line of Connecticut cabinet makers.

Simeon married Elizabeth (Welles) (1780-1828) on May 21, 1797 at Wethersfield, CT.[2] In the 1790s Simeon was living in New York City partnered with William Mills in the firm of Deming and Mills, doing business at *"No. 374 Queen Street, two doors above the Friends Meeting, New York."* One of the cabinetmaking firm's labels is shown in **Figure 151**.[3]

While at New York City, the firm produced what has been termed by some experts as one of the finest American sideboards ever made (*see Figure 152*).

This sideboard was made for Oliver Wolcott, Sr. (1726-1797), signer of the Declaration of Independence, U.S. Comptroller and Secretary of the Treasury under George Washington, and first Governor of the State of Connecticut. The sideboard is part of the collection of the National Gallery of Art in Washington, D.C.[4]

....

Israel Sack described the sideboard as follows:

"Hepplewhite mahogany and satinwood serpentine-front sideboard, a masterpiece of inlayer's art. The cupboard doors are inlaid with drapery and tassel motifs centered by inlaid urns, a drapery chain of tinted inlaid bellflowers interlace with the drapery and tassel inlay of the center cupboard and is repeated on the bowed center drawer, the drawer and cupboard doors are bordered by green tinted crossbanding with fan-inlaid quadrants in the corners; the tapered legs are inlaid with tinted bellflowers and interlaced loops, the original label of Mills & Deming is behind the right hand cupboard door."[5]

....

Figure 151

Label from the firm of Mills (William) & Deming (Simeon) at New York City ca. 1793-1798.

"Makes and sells, all kinds of Cabinet Furniture and Chairs, after the most modern fashions and on reasonable terms."

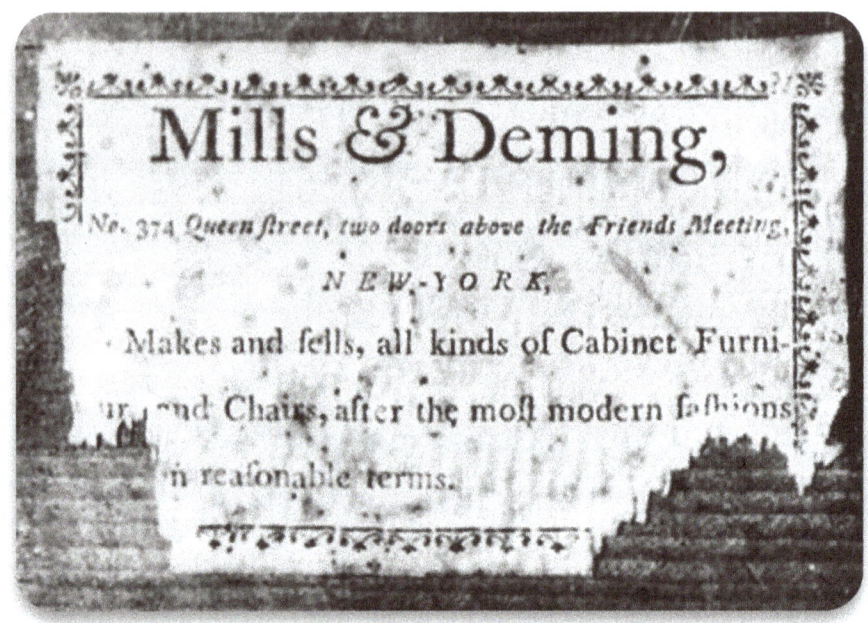

Figure 152

Hepplewhite sideboard by Mills & Deming, NYC (ca. 1793-1798), part of the permanent collection of the National Gallery of Art, Washington.

Source: Yale University Library Digital Collection Federal Furniture

After leaving New York, Deming worked at Stockbridge, MA, for a time, and moved to East Bloomfield, NY, in 1813, where he purchased property, continued his cabinetmaking, and farmed. One history states: *"He was a cabinetmaker by trade, and was considered a very fine workman. After his removal to Bloomfield in 1813 he started farming, which he continued for the rest of his life. He was quite aristocratic in his ideas, and his wife was a woman of elegant manners."*[6]

The pair had eight children, only one of whom (Adelia, 1816-1818) was born at East Bloomfield. Simeon's son William (1802-1889) identified in *Census* records as a farmer, lived with his father on the homestead at East Bloomfield and carried on there after Simeon's passing in 1855.[7]

The East Bloomfield Historical Society has exhibited a wonderful Simeon Deming sideboard produced during his tenure in the town (**see Figure 153**).

Showing clear Empire influences, the sideboard features turned legs, rich crotch mahogany veneer and flame birch or flame maple inlaid decorations, and supports Deming's standing as a superb furniture maker. Note the use of white glass drawer pulls.[8]

At East Bloomfield, Simeon Deming lived about ½ mile east of, and on the same road as, the late 1820s to 1835 Abner Jones property, on today's Gauss Rd.[9]

Lacking any clear attributions to date, we cannot absolutely prove that Simeon Deming was the source of Abner Jones' remarkable shelf clock cases. However, we can definitely say that he is the leading candidate, as his other extant works certainly exhibit the talent to qualify him as such.

---

[1] 1820 U.S. Census for Bloomfield, NY; Ontario County Deeds, Book 41, p. 541; Ontario County Deeds, Book 46, p. 7; Ontario County Deeds, Book 41, p. 540; Ontario County Deeds, Book 41, p. 539; Ontario County Deeds, Book 60, p. 167.

[2] Deming, Judson Keith, Editor. *Genealogy of the Descendants of John Deming of Wethersfield, CT,* Goolebooks.com, 1904, pp. 115-117.

[3] Yale University Library Collection – Federal Furniture. findit.library.yale,edu/catalog/digcoll:1025155.

[4] Ibid.

[5] Ibid.

[6] Deming. p. 115.

[7] Deming. p. 115; *1820-1850 U.S. Census for Bloomfield and East Bloomfield, NY*

[8] Correspondence with Robert Cheney.

[9] *1830 U.S. Census for Bloomfield, NY.*

Figure 153

Simeon Deming, East Bloomfield, NY, sideboard. When the photo was taken, the piece was on loan to the East Bloomfield, NY, Historical Society.

CHAPTER EIGHT

Late Cornice Top Cases Without Drawers

When the author began his attempt to piece together the Abner Jones shelf clock case chronology, it was hoped (and perhaps even assumed) that an analysis of the extant case styles combined with the available clocks with numbered movements would yield the ability to line up the case styles by production sequence. Things have not turned out that way.

As noted previously, the clocks made from 1835 on do not appear to have been produced in distinct groups, but as a mixture of styles and elements over time, suggesting, perhaps, that cases could have been made to order to meet the individual preference of the prospective buyer.

So as we move forward we will follow the variation in case styles collectors have encountered and appreciated over the years while tracking the movement numbers when and where they appear. Attempting to apply organization/order/sequence to the remaining array of Abner Jones shelf clocks made between 1835 and 1841 is a desirable approach but, as we will see, a bit of nuance is required in order to make it succeed. The primary obstacle relates to the fact that with the exception of the *Group Four Carved Scroll Top Cases*, all of Abner Jones' late shelf clocks (i.e., all of the rest of the clocks we will examine) have cornice tops, a classic Empire furniture element, but a challenge when one hopes to differentiate between our remaining examples. A close examination of the cases from this period yielded just enough differences to give the author an opening.

Part One: Group Five – Sloped Cornice Top Shelf Cases Without Drawers

We start with the case type descriptively termed the *Sloped Cornice Top Cases* and discussed as part of **Group Five**. The name refers to the style of molded cornice top found on many of the post-1835 Jones cases in an attempt to distinguish these cases from those with what the author has chosen to term **Sharp Cornice Tops**. The differences can be seen in *Figures 154 and 155* below. None of the clocks included here in **Group Five** have drawers, and all have carved half columns. In the interest of full disclosure, there are, in fact, some sloped cornice top cases with drawers, but we will examine them as part of another group.

Only one of the currently known **Group Five** clocks has a movement with a stamped number. That number, #48, is the lowest movement number found on any of the known Abner Jones clocks yet to be examined in this work.

The **Group Five** cases come in at least three sizes, creatively identified by the author as the "large," "medium," and "small." With Abner Jones, "large" always means very large compared with almost any other shelf clock produced in America in the 1830s, and the terms "medium" and "small" are terms relative only to other Jones cases.

Clock 5-A is of the "large" variety. The **height of the case measures 46¾", the width at the base 19½", the width at the cornice top 23¾", the depth in the main**

Figures 154 & 155

Figure 154 (top) Each of the Group Five Clocks have molded tops with this sloping form.
Figure 155 (bottom) Many of the Abner Jones shelf clocks have this sharp edged cornice form.
They will be discussed as part of the Group Six examples below.

Figures 156

Location of the home and shop of A.C. Totman at East Bloomfield ca. 1859.

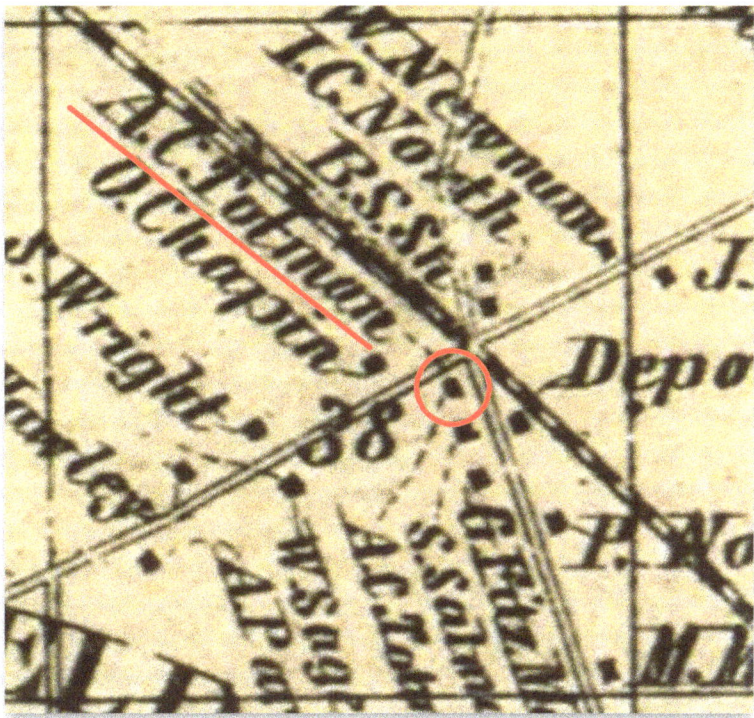

case 6⅞" and the depth of the cornice top is 8⅜". The mahogany half columns are decorated in a complex pattern of carved and turned elements. Note, as always, that dimensions will differ slightly between similar cases. *Clock 5-A* is shown in **Figure 157**. The door features an open brass pull.

A.C. Totman – The Abner Jones Clock Repairer of Record

Clock 5-A contains a long list of repair dates written in pencil on the back of the door, along with a number of other interesting notations. Prominent among the recordings is a repair date stating, **"Put in order January, 1880 / A. C. Totman"** found on the upper inside door panel. This is just one of the repair notations by Asahel C. Totman found in a dozen or more surviving Abner Jones clocks. Totman was an interesting figure in his own right.

Born in Saratoga, NY, in 1821, Totman received training in the clock and watch trade and relocated to Plymouth Hollow, CT, as a young man to work for the Seth Thomas company. For several years in the late 1840s and early 1850s, he served as Superintendent of the clock factory. He relocated to East Bloomfield before 1860, where he was listed in the *1860 Census* as a "Clockmaker." Totman enlisted in the Union Army's 65th Regiment of the New York Infantry in September, 1864. Histories note that he was present at Appomattox for Lee's surrender to Grant and was discharged in July, 1865. *Census* listings in 1870 and 1875 described him as a "Clock Repairer."[1]

Totman died at age 67 on April 3, 1889. The location of his house, which also served as his shop, is shown in **Figure 156** from the 1859 *Beers Map of Ontario County* at the four corners in the village of East Bloomfield.[2] A parking lot and bank are now located on the site, but the corner appropriately features a modern replica of a street clock.

There are additional notations on the back board of the door of *Clock 5-A*, including much of the clock's history, as follows: **"Bought at Peter Covert's(sp?) / Sale April 25, 1896/ D.C. Wheeler,"** then **"D.C. Wheeler gave to JS Kinman May 24, 1900 / Jennie Kinman gave to John Whitiker July 4, 1928 / Given to Esther and Clara Wyckoff 1950 / Repaired by Stephan Illes – Ithaca N.Y. / June 9, 1950 /** and **/ Cleaned Harold Royce 12/8/66."** Messrs. Illes and Royce were known to the author and were wonderful gentlemen. At some point thereafter, the clock passed into the possession of noted collector Peter Zaharis of Ithaca, NY. It later sold at auction and even later was donated to the East Bloomfield, NY, Historical Society by benefactor Paul Hudson of East Bloomfield.

Figure 157

Clock 5-A in the collection of the East Bloomfield, NY, Historical Society.
This is an example of the largest of the Group Five cases.

94 • *Without Equal: The Clocks of Abner Jones of Bloomfield, New York*

The movement in *Clock 5-A* has the number "**48**" stamped in the "usual" location on the right front of the back plate, as shown in **Figure 158**. Also of interest is the additional stamping of our ubiquitous "4" or "7" positioned sideways and above the "48." A miss-hit of an intended number "4"? Something else? Just another question!

Clock 5-A has a well-preserved original dial with seconds bit as shown in **Figure 159**.

Our example of the "Medium-sized" **Group Five** cases, *Clock 5-C*, is shown in **Figure 160**. This clock is now part of the collection of the Hoffman Clock Museum, Newark, NY. Our "Small" Group Five example is Clock 5-D shown in **Figures 161 and 162**.

Figures 158 & 159

Figure 158 (top): The movement of Clock 5-A showing the stamped number "48" with either a "4" or "7" stamped sideways just above. Figure 159 (bottom): The well-preserved original dial of Clock 5-A.

Figure 160

Clock 5-C, representative of the "Medium-Sized" cases in Group Five. From the collection of the Hoffman Clock Museum, Newark, NY.

Figure 161

Clock 5-D, *representing the smallest of the Group Five case examples.*

Photo Courtesy Cottone's Auctions

Chapter Eight • 97

Figure 162

The fine, original dial found on Clock 5-D.

Photo Courtesy Cottone's Auctions

The "medium" cases measure approximately 40⅜" high, 19⅜" wide at the base, 23⅞" wide at the top board, 6¾" deep in the case and 8⅞" deep at the top board. The carved and turned columns are excellent. The dial has been accurately restored. The movement is not numbered. This clock has an open brass door pull similar to that found on *Clock 5-A*.

Clock 5-D (Figure 161), our "small" example, measures 36" in height, 17" wide at the base and 21¼" wide at the top board, 6⅞" deep in the case and 8" deep at the top board. This case has wonderfully carved and turned columns and a solid, round brass door pull. The movement of this clock is not numbered. The fine, original dial of *Clock 5-D* is shown in **Figure 162**.

Our final Group Five, slope-top cornice example, *Clock 5-E*, is shown in **Figure 163**. This, by all appearances, is a well-preserved, medium-sized case with an original dial with colorful spandrels with a shell motif. This clock was once owned by Doug Blazey of Victor, NY, and sold at auction after his passing in 1996. It was featured in the display entitled **"Horological Rarities of Space City '99"** at the 1999 NAWCC National Convention at Houston, TX.[3] The author has been unable to locate the clock for further examination.

For a detailed comparison of all of the Group Five clocks, see Appendix E.

Figure 163

Clock 5-E, *current ownership unknown, shown as displayed at the* 1990 NAWCC National Convention *exhibit at Houston, TX.*

Figure 164
Clock 6-A is representative of the largest of the Group Six clocks.

Part Two: Group Six – Sharp Cornice Top Shelf Cases Without Drawers

Group Six features cases with the *sharp cornice tops* shown in **Figure 155**. As with the **Group Five** clocks, those in this group come in several sizes, but the variations in this group are more extensive than those in **Group Five**, and the number of extant clocks is significantly higher, perhaps suggesting that more of this style case were produced.

Our first **Group Six** clock, *Clock 6-A* is shown in **Figure 164**. *Clock 6-A* is of the "large" variety.

The **height of the case measures 46", the width at the base 20½", the width at the cornice top 24¾", the depth of the main case 7" and the depth of the cornice top is 8⅜"**. The mahogany half columns are decorated in a complex pattern of carved and turned elements.

Note, as always, that dimensions will differ slightly between similar cases. The door features a brass pull and a push-button door release.

Clock 6-A is one of two Abner Jones shelf clocks found to date with a number stamped not on the movement but *on the pendulum bob*, and the bob on this clock is stamped with the number **#90**, as shown in **Figure 165**. This movement is only one of a select few featuring the planetary winding gear feature on the time side winding drum that makes it easier to wind the clock, as discussed in **Chapter Three**. A photo of the time side great wheel arbor showing the internal planetary gearing is shown in **Figure 166**.

Remarkably, the other clock with a numbered pendulum bob is the same model as Clock 6-A and both are currently owned by the same family.

The clock with number **#91**, *Clock 6-B*, is shown in **Figure 167**. As with *Clock 6-A*, this movement does incorporate the planetary gearing option. Minor differences between this clock and the former include variations in the decorative dial spandrels.

Clock 6-B is also of the "large" variety. The **height of the case measures 45⅞", the width at the base 20⅝", the width at the cornice top 24¾", the depth of the main case 6⅞" and the depth of the cornice top is 8¼"**. While this clock is virtually identical to *Clock 6-A*, we nonetheless note the slight differences in the dimensions of the two cases. The door features a brass pull and a push-button door release.

The wonderfully decorated dial of *Clock 6-B* is shown in **Figure 168**, with a close-up of the shell motif spandrel in **Figure 169**.

Figures 165 & 166

Figure 165 (left): The back of the pendulum bob of Clock 6-A *showing the stamped number "90." This is one of two clocks found so far numbered in this fashion. Figure 166 (right): A close-up of the time side great wheel of* Clock 6-A *showing details of the planetary winding gear feature.*

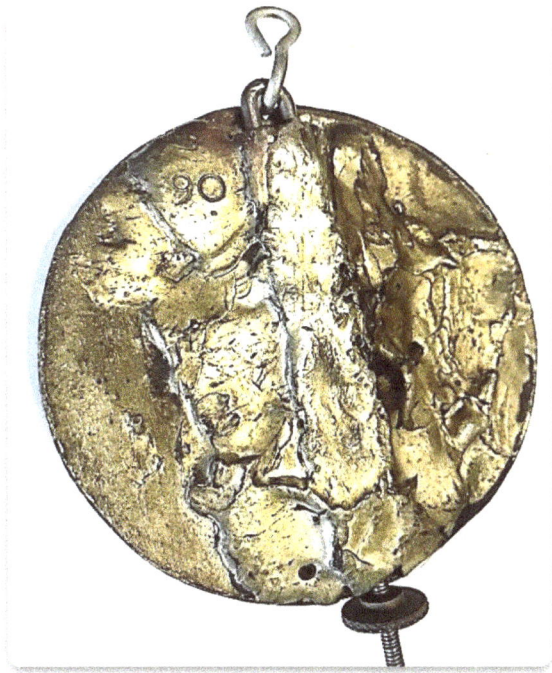 

Photo Courtesy Evan Edwards

Figure 167
Clock 6-B is a sibling to Clock 6-A, and carries a consecutive movement number with that clock.

Figures 168 & 169

Figure 168 (top): The original dial of Clock 6-B.

Figure 169 (bottom): Close-up of the fine folk-art decorative shell motif found on the dial of Clock 6-B.

The numbered pendulum bob of *Clock 6-B* is shown in **Figures 170 and 171**, and other pictured details include the open brass door pull (*see Figure 172*) and push-button door latch elements (*see Figure 173*).

The **Group Six** clock with the lowest recorded movement number is *Clock 6-C*, shown in **Figure 174**.

A photo of the movement of the clock, stamped with the number "**50**," is shown in **Figure 175**.

Figures 176 and 177 show details of the door closure mechanism found on *Clock 6-C*.

This "medium" case and other extant clocks like it measure (approximately) **40" high, 20½" wide at the base, 24-25" wide at the top board, 6¾" deep in the case and 9" deep at the top board.** This clock has a well-preserved original dial, no door pull and a spring-loaded latch door release.

Figures 170 & 171

Figures 170 (left) and 171 (right) showing the pewter-filled back and the brass casing of the numbered #91 pendulum bob of Clock 6-B.

Figures 172 & 173

Figure 172 (left): The cast brass open door pull found on Clocks 6-A and 6-B.
Figure 173 (right): Details of the push-button door release found on both clocks.

Figure 174
The "Medium" sized case of Clock 6-C.

Figure 175
The movement of Clock 6-C showing the stamped number "50."

Figure 176
Showing the door edge and the spring-loaded door latch found on many of the Abner Jones shelf clocks.

Figure 177
Showing the inside of the door and the steel spring used to press the latch in place when closed.

Chapter Eight • 105

Figure 178

Clock 6-D, the carved column and cornice top shelf clock now in the collection of the Ontario County (NY) Historical Society.

Photo Courtesy Evan Edwards

Figure 179

The inscription, in the hand of repairman A.C. Totman of East Bloomfield, stating "Abner Jones Maker" found in Clock 6-D.

106 • Without Equal: The Clocks of Abner Jones of Bloomfield, New York

Clock 6-D is shown in **Figure 178**. This clock was passed down over the years in the Steele and Hamlin families of East Bloomfield, NY, and is now in the collection of the Ontario County (NY) Historical Society. This is a near-duplicate of *Clock 6-C* but it does not have a numbered movement. The case has a glass door pull and a simple hook-and-eye latch on the door.

The board covering the mirror on the back of the door of *Clock 6-D* retains a long list of repair notations penned by East Bloomfield repairman A.C. Totman, plus the statement, courtesy of Totman, *"Abner Jones Maker"* (*see* **Figure 179**). This is one of the few written attributions found on any Abner Jones shelf clock, albeit not penned by him.

Clock 6-E (*see Figure 180*) is otherwise similar to *Clocks 6-C* and *6-D* with the exception that it has a dial with **Arabic** numerals, *making this clock the only post-1835 Abner Jones shelf clock found to date with this feature*. As noted previously, all of the **Group Two** clocks had dials with Arabic numerals, but all of the Jones shelf clocks thereafter apparently featured dials with Roman numerals – except this clock.

Evan Edwards recorded and photographed this clock in the collection of Doug Blazey of Victor, NY. The clock was sold in the 1996 Blazey auction. The whereabouts of this clock is not known today so it has not been examined by the author. Edwards recorded that the movement of this clock was stamped with the number "**64**."

Figure 180

Note the dial with Arabic numerals, a feature rarely seen on Abner Jones' post-1835 clocks.

Photo Courtesy Evan Edwards

Our next three **Group Six** clocks feature *turned columns* in place of the carved columns found on clocks **6-A through 6-E**. Otherwise they are similar in size to cases **6-C through 6-E**.

Clock 6-F is shown in **Figure 181**. When this clock was investigated by Evan Edwards it was one of the many clocks in the renowned collection of the late Tony Sposato of New York. It was sold in 1986,[4] and its current ownership is not known, although it did appear in an exhibit at the 1999 NAWCC National Convention in Houston, TX.[5] Views of the movement of this clock, with the stamped number "**56**," are shown in **Figures 182 and 183**. This movement does have the addition of the planetary winding gear arrangement on the time side great wheel.

Figures 182 & 183
Top and Below, respectively, showing the movement of Clock 6-F and a close-up of the stamped number "56."

Figure 181
Shelf Clock 6-F is similar in size to the other Group Six cases but has turned rather than carved columns. This is the clock as featured in the Richard A. Bourne Co. auction catalog for the Anthony Sposato collection sale in 1986.

Photos Courtesy Evan Edwards

108 • *Without Equal: The Clocks of Abner Jones of Bloomfield, New York*

Two additional Group Six clocks with turned columns are known. *Clock 6-G*, as shown in **Figure 184**, was recorded by Evan Edwards in the collection of the late Henry Sayward, an early afficionado of upstate New York clocks. Current ownership of this clock is not known, and the clock has not been examined by the author.

The wood door panel with round glass insert is an interesting adaptation but appears from the photo likely not to be original.

Our third extant **Group Six** clock with turned columns, *Clock 6-H*, is shown in **Figure 185**. It is one of several Abner Jones shelf clocks once in the collection of Henry (Hank) Stegeman of Rochester, NY.

A fine example of the turned column variety, it contains a movement with the stamped number "**87**" as shown in **Figure 186**.

Figure 184

Clock 6-G, *a turned column and cornice case with a wooden lower door panel that appears to have been installed in place of the original mirror.*

Photo Courtesy Evan Edwards

Figure 185

Turned column and cornice Clock 6-H *containing movement #87.*

Figure 186

The movement stamped #87 *contained in Clock 6-H.*

Chapter Eight • 109

Our next, and last, **Group Six** clock, *Clock 6-I*, shown in *Figure 187*, is a return to the carved column, cornice top, "medium" sized case category. It was selected to be the last clock reviewed in this group because of several important characteristics.

First, *this clock contains the second-highest numbered movement, #95, found to date in any Abner Jones shelf clock*. We will recall the detailed discussion in **Chapter Three** of *Clock 1-B*, a clock with what appears to be one of the earliest shelf clock cases made by Abner Jones. We also recall that this early case contains a time-and-strike movement not with a very low number, but a movement with the number **#96**, the highest number found to date in any Abner Jones shelf clock. Lastly, we remember that movement **#96**, with its many extra turnings and decorative embellishments, is one of the most unique Abner Jones movements ever seen.

Movement **#96** brings movement **#95** into extra focus in terms of answering the question *"Were the two made sequentially?"* Evidence suggests that they were, because in addition to the stamped movement numbers 95 and 96, both contain additional sequential numbers stamped onto the movements, both in similar locations on the lower right side of the front of the back plate. *On Clock 6-I, movement #95, the number stamped there is #16*, and on **Clock 1-B**, *movement #96, the number stamped there is #17*. The significance of these sequential numbers is unclear. Nonetheless, the existence of this "extra" set of numbers supports the conclusion that both are late, very late, movements. Why one is in a post-1835 case and the other, with special features for a clearly special purpose, shows up in what appears to be one of the earliest cases made by Jones remains an open question.

―――――――― *Figure 187* ――――――――

Clock 6-I, *which contains the next-to-highest numbered movement found to date in an Abner Jones shelf clock.*

―――――――― *Figures 188 & 189* ――――――――

Figures 188 *(top)* and 189 *(bottom) showing, respectively, the movement and dial, and the stamped number "95" found on the movement of* Clock 6-I.

Photos Courtesy Evan Edwards

The photo in *Figure 187* was taken, and the movement information recorded, by Evan Edwards in the exhibit room at the Chicago, IL, NAWCC National Convention in 1992. The whereabouts of this clock are not known to the author.

The clock's inner dial has been painted gold. It appears to be repainted, but without further examination it is not possible to absolutely determine this. The dial has a seconds bit.

Edwards' note on the back of the photo states, *"95 stamped on mvt rear plate / 16 on lower right rear plate / on exhibit at Chicago National mtg."* Close-up photos of movement #95 are shown in **Figures 188 and 189**.

For a detailed comparison of all of the Group Six clocks, see Appendix F.

---

[1] The material on A.C. Totman was provided to the author by collector John Fadden. John received the material from Don Mansfield, a member of the East Bloomfield Historical Society. John and Mr. Mansfield have our thanks. Sources include the following: *1860, 1870, and 1875 U.S. Census for Bloomfield, NY*; http://history.goerie.com/today-in-erie-history-april-19-1903.; http://www.newyorkroots.ort/ontario/militaryWESTBewsoldiers.; FindAGrave.com/Asahel C. Totman; http://ontario.nygenweb.net/toobituaries; *History of Ontario Co. New York*. Everts, Ensign & Everts, Philadelphia, PA, 1878, p. 222; familytreemaker.genealogy.com/users/s/h/e/Cornelius-T-Shea/AsahelTotman; Records of the East Bloomfield, NY, Cemetery, East Bloomfield Historical Society.

[2] Beers, D.G. *Map of Ontario County, New York,1859*, A.R.Z. Dawson Publishing Co., Philadelphia, PA., 1859.

[3] 1999 NAWCC National Convention Commemorative Exhibit Catalogue. *Horological Rarities of Space City '99*, p. 24.

[4] Richard A. Bourne Co. Auction catalog for the *"Rare Clock Collection of Anthony Sposato*, January 7, 1986.

[5] 1999 NAWCC National Convention Commemorative Exhibit Catalogue. *Horological Rarities of Space City '99*, p. 26.

CHAPTER NINE

Late Cornice Top Cases with Drawers

Lower cabinet sections with drawers were the primary feature of all of the early Abner Jones shelf clocks, as represented by the **Group One** and **Group Two** models. Contemporary with the move to West Bloomfield in 1835, case styles took a fundamental move away from the cabinet drawers component, but this design feature never quite went away, as we will see.

Incorporating components from late carved and turned half column and cornice models, the great tradition continued. Our first examples are included in what we will call the **Group Seven** clocks.

Part One: The Group Seven Clocks

Clock 7-A, shown in **Figure 190**, features carved half columns and a sharp cornice, with the traditional Jones

Figure 190

Clock 7-A *features a late version of the signature Abner Jones lower cabinet section with three drawers.*

112 • *Without Equal: The Clocks of Abner Jones of Bloomfield, New York*

three-drawer lower cabinet treatment. The lower full-width drawer front is rounded.

The clock measures 45" tall, 22¾" wide and 8⅞" deep at the cornice top; 18½" wide and 7⅛" deep at the cabinet base; and 17" wide and 6¾" deep at the main case. The feet are 3" in height.

This is a fine, original clock that for most of its life resided with the Parmele family of East Bloomfield. The case has glass drawer pulls, a brass door pull and a spring-loaded press tab door release.

The inner dial features a recessed brass seconds bit, and the dial spandrels are decorated with a colorful if somewhat primitive shell motif, similar to those seen on several other clocks, including *Clocks 4-C and 6-E*.

The movement of *Clock 7-A* is numbered **#57** and the number/symbol "7" appears on the front of the back plate below the time side great wheel. The meaning and/or purpose of the additional "7" stamp is unknown (*see Figures 191a-c*). The clock's original dial is shown in **Figure 192**.

The interior of *Clock 7-A*, quite typical of all late Abner Jones cases, is shown in **Figure 193**. The square cast iron weights shown with this clock are one of the two varieties most often seen on the Jones shelf clocks.

Figure 191a

The movement of Clock 7-A showing the number "57" stamped on the front of the movement back plate.

Figures 191b & 191c

Figure 191b (top), showing the movement number, in close-up, and Figure 191c (bottom), showing the number/symbol "7", which appears on the front of the back plate below the time side great wheel.

Figure 192

The fine, original dial of Clock 7-A, showing a variation of the "shell" motif in the spandrels.

Chapter Nine • 113

Figure 193
The interior of Clock 7-A showing the typical compound pulleys and cast iron weights.

Photo Courtesy Chris Tahk

Our second **Group Seven** example is *Clock 7-B* as shown in *Figure 194*.

The clock is essentially a medium **Group Six** carved half column and sharp cornice base case with a single flat-front drawer cabinet base and paw feet added.

The door release is by push-button, and, when pictured, the door pull was missing from the clock. The drawer pulls appear to be wood in the picture, originality uncertain. The dial appears to be well preserved and original.

When photographed by Evan Edwards, the clock was in the collection of the late Doug Blazey of Victor, NY. The movement in *Clock 7-B* is numbered **#65** as shown in *Figure 195*.

Clock 7-C, shown in *Figure 196*, is yet another carved half column and sharp cornice case with three-drawer base. This was Evan Edwards' personal clock which he stated he had purchased at an auction at Lebanon, New Hampshire in the 1970s.[1]

Figures 194 & 195

Figure 194 (left): Clock 7-B is essentially a medium Group Six clock with added one-drawer cabinet base and paw feet.
Figure 195 (right): The movement of Clock 7-B showing the number "65" stamped on the front of the back plate.

Photo Courtesy Evan Edwards

Photo Courtesy Evan Edwards

Chapter Nine • 115

Figure 196

The handsome and original Group Seven Clock 7-C.

Photo Courtesy Cottone's Auctions

The fine original dial of *Clock 7-C* featuring simplified floral decorations in the spandrels is shown in **Figure 197**. It also incorporates a recessed brass seconds bit. The drawer pulls are glass and of two sizes, and there is no door pull. The door has a spring-loaded press tab latch.

Clock 7-D is the last of the Abner Jones late cornice-top cases with drawers identified to date by the author (***see Figure 198***). It is of the same relative size as *Clocks 7-A and C*, but features turned columns instead of carved. This clock was once in the collection of Doug Blazey of Victor, NY, and was the cover clock on the auction pamphlet when his clocks were sold following his death in 1996.

Within the cabinet section, the lower, rounded front drawer has likely replaced wood pulls, and the two upper flat front drawers are key-open only. The door has a glass pull, possibly original. The clock has what appears to be a well-preserved dial with floral decorations in the spandrels.

Like Scroll Top *Clock 4-G*, this clock employs a very unusual, for Abner Jones, method of attaching the movement to the backboard. An examination of the three extant clocks with this anomaly is provided in **Chapter Ten**. Also unusual, compared to virtually all of the other post-1835 Jones clocks, is the fact that this case has wallpaper on the backboard that appears, at least from the extant pictures, to be original (***see Figure 199***). This wallpaper does not match the print found in the **Group One** and **Group Two** clocks previously examined. *Clock 7-D* was sold to a new owner in 1996 and to date the author has been unable to ascertain the identity of the current owner or to examine the clock for other details.

For a detailed comparison of all of the Group Seven clocks, see Appendix H.

Figure 197

The fine original dial of Clock 7-C *features a recessed seconds bit and floral decorations in the dial spandrels.*

Photo Courtesy Cottone's Auctions

Figure 198

Clock 7-D, with turned columns, sharp cornice top and a three-drawer cabinet base.

Photo Courtesy Evan Edwards

Figure 199

Clock 7-D has what appears to be original wallpaper on the backboard, an unusual feature for a post-1835 Abner Jones clock. What appears to be a repair label is pasted in the center of the case.

Photo Courtesy Evan Edwards

Part Two: The Group Eight Clocks

Within the general definition of "*Late Cornice Top Cases With Drawers*," there are two distinct groupings of clocks, thus *Part One* and *Part Two*. The Part One, or **Group Seven**, cases are, as noted, combinations of late shelf clocks with added cabinet sections, all reminiscent of the earliest Abner Jones shelf clock cases with drawers. As the base cases *sans* drawers were already "large," adding cabinet sections yielded formidable overall heights of approximately 45" including feet.

Figures 200 & 201

Figure 200 (left): Clock 8-A is the only one of the three documented Group Eight clocks to feature complex turned half columns. Note the turned feet, four cabinet drawers and sharp cornice top, all characteristic of this case style.
Figure 201 (right): The original drawer pulls found on Clock 8-A and the other Group Eight clocks are these bulbous clear glass knobs.

Photos Courtesy Cottone's Auctions

Figure 202

Clock 8-A *showing the interior view of the movement, inner dial, bell, pulleys, pendulum bob and the weights.*

Photo Courtesy Cottone's Auctions

Our *Part Two* group, designated as the clocks of **Group Eight**, are quite literally *huge* cases with sharp cornice tops and drawers, but are of a distinctive design with a taller central case and a cabinet section with *four* drawers. The dials measure 14" square, the largest found on any Jones shelf model. In addition, each of the documented **Group Eight** clocks have dials decorated very differently from any others reviewed to date, perhaps indicating that a different dial artist was at work on these presumed *late* clocks.

The fact that only three of these clocks have been documented to date underscores the rarity of this model.

Overall, the **Group Eight** clocks **measure** (*approximately, as always*) **55" in height, 26" wide and 9" deep at the cornice; 24" wide, 9" high and 8" deep at the cabinet base, and 19½" wide and 7" deep in the center of the case.** With the possible exception of *Clock 3-A* which, as we recall, is missing its original paw feet so that its original height can only be estimated, **these are the tallest Abner Jones shelf clock models yet identified**.

Chapter Nine • 121

Figures 203 & 204

Figure 203 (top): Clock 8-A and each of the other clocks in this group feature dial decorations unlike those found on any of the other Abner Jones shelf clocks reviewed so far. Each includes simplified flowers in red, pink, white or blue and stems and leaves in green and yellow. Figure 204 (bottom): A close-up view of the floral decorations in the spandrels of Clock 8-A.

Each of our **Group Eight** clocks appears with original, bulbous, clear glass drawer pulls. Only one of the clocks features a pull on the door, and all use simple hook-and-eye latches to secure the doors. All of the clocks have turned, rather than carved paw, feet.

The first **Group Eight** clock to be examined is *Clock 8-A*, shown in **Figure 200**. This clock appeared in a New York auction in 2006 consigned from the collection of Alfred Burnham of Connecticut, and then again in 2018 from a Florida collection. This is the only one of the three known **Group Eight** examples to feature complex turnings on the columns. Otherwise, the basic elements of turned feet, four cabinet drawers (the lower two of which have rounded fronts), thin, tall half columns and sharp cornice tops are evident.

Figure 201 provides a close-up of the drawer pulls found on the three **Group Eight** clocks, and *Figure 202* shows an interior view of *Clock 8-A*.

Figures 203 and 204 provide detailed views of the dial of *Clock 8-A*, and in particular the very simplified decorations of flowers and greens found on each of the **Group Eight** clocks.

The movement of *Clock 8-A* is not numbered.

Our next clock, *Clock 8-B*, is shown in **Figure 205**. This is yet another Abner Jones clock that has spent its life with one extended family, a history detailed below.

This is a fine, original example of this group, and this and the remaining clock each feature round turned half columns with simple turnings only at the top and base. The movement of this clock is not numbered.

While the other **Group Eight** clocks appear to locate the simple hook-and-eye door latch adjacent to the mullion between the upper dial glass and lower door mirror, the latch on *Clock 8-B* is near the very top of the door. The implication for anyone attempting to simply open the door to wind these clocks should be examined. First, consider the fact that this and the other Abner Jones clocks were utilized most generally as mantel clocks. The fashionable Greek Revival homes of the period tended to offer ceiling heights of 10' and up, which was a good thing, as a typical mantel height of perhaps 48"-50" inches plus a standard **Group Eight** case of 54", added up to between 8½' and 9'! Therefore, it would appear evident that to wind such a clock sitting on any standard mantel in the age in which it was built would have required the use of a large step ladder on a weekly basis.

Detail of the dial spandrel decoration on *Clock 8-B* is shown in **Figure 206**.

Figure 207 shows *Clock 8-C*, a clock once owned by Henry (Hank) Stegeman of Rochester, NY, and later part of the notable collection of the late Pete Zaharis of Ithaca, NY. The history of the clock prior to Stegeman is not known, and while the clock did sell at auction in 1997, its current ownership could not be determined by the author.

This clock is a near duplicate of *Clock 8-B*, with the exception of the rosettes found on the lower door blocks. This is the only one of the three **Group Eight** clocks with a door pull, this in cast brass, and the only one with a **numbered movement (88)**.

The decorations in the dial spandrels are again of flowers – in this example in blue and pink – and greens.

For a detailed comparison of all of the Group Eight clocks, see Appendix H.

---

[1] Edwards, Evan. *Abner Jones Clockmaker* (unpublished manuscript, August 1982).

CLOCK 8-B: THE BACK STORY

The history of this clock can be traced back to Edward H. Morse (1816-1901) of Canandaigua, NY. His son John (1850-1943) and wife Ida (1868-1945), who were residents of East Bloomfield, NY, in the late 1800s, inherited the clock, and then passed it on to their daughter Mabel (1902-1999), who married Louis H. Converse of Clifton Springs, Ontario County, NY. The clock next went into the possession of Mabel and Louis's daughter Ruth Converse (1922-2017), who married Robert Pierce (1915-2002) in 1939. When Ruth passed away in 2017, the clock was inherited by her first granddaughter, Kathy Willson Bowerman. Ruth was predeceased by Kathy's mother, Ruth's first daughter, Carolyn Pierce (1941-2014), who married Harold Willson (1941-2014) in 1960. One interesting aspect of this line of ownership is that from the third transition of ownership on, the clock has, by family tradition, been handed down to daughters, not sons, of the owners.

Figures 205 & 206

Figure 205 (left): Clock 8-B which has spent its life with one family, originally from the Bloomfield, NY, area.
Figure 206 (right): Detail of the decorated spandrels on Clock 8-B; similar to that seen on the other Group Eight clocks but with white flowers.

Photo Courtesy Evan Edwards

Photo Courtesy Kathleen Bowerman

Figure 207
A full case view of Clock 8-C.

Photo Courtesy Cottone's Auctions

Chapter Nine • 125

CHAPTER TEN

Basics, Anomalies and Speculations

In **Chapter Ten** we will seek to survey basic information on and characteristics of the various components that make up Abner Jones' shelf clocks while extending a few speculative musings when appropriate. The topics start with movement basics and move on in an arguably random order!

Movement Gear Counts:

Figure 208 is a chart showing the time-and-strike train gear counts from one Abner Jones tall clock and a sampling of shelf clocks. One area of interest is the question of whether there are variations, significant or minor, from movement to movement and, if so, the effect of those

---

Figure 208

Abner Jones Movement Comparisons

STRIKE SIDE GEARS

CLOCK	GREAT	2ND	3RD	4TH	FLY
TALL CLOCK:					
OCHS	84t	72t/8p	48t/6p	48t/6p	6p
SHELF CLOCKS:					
1-A	Timepiece — No strike train!				
1-J	78t	56t/8p	56t/7p	36t/7p	7p
2-H	(Strike side details not reported)				
3-B	78t	56t/8p	56t/7p	42t/7p	7p
4-N	78t	56t/8p	56t/7p	42t/7p	7p
LM-1	78t	56t/8p	56t/7p	42t/7p	7p

TIME SIDE GEARS

CLOCK	GREAT	2ND	3RD	ESCAPE	MOTION WORK	EST. PEND. LENGTH**
TALL CLOCK:						
OCHS	96t	56t/8p	56t/8p	36t/8p	Hour 72t; Intermediate 36t/6p Minute 36t	40.75"
SHELF CLOCKS:						
1-A (TP)	96t	60t/8p	60t/8p	39t/7p	Same...	20.17"
1-J	96t	60t/8p	60t/8p	39t/7p	Same...	20.17"
2-H	96t	60t/8p	60t/8p	39t/7p*	Same...	20.17"
3-B	96t	60t/8p	56t/8p	39t/7p	Same...	23.16"
4-N	96t	80t/8p	56t/8p	39t/7p	Same...	27.18"
LM-1	96t	60t/8p	60t/8p	42t/7p	Same...	17.39

*Corrected from old report, count re-verified.
**Courtesy of and with thanks to Chris Tahk.

Note: The clock designated **LM-1** above is actually a loose movement and it is a captivating curiosity. This movement is discussed at length later in this chapter. **LM-1** has the shortest computed pendulum length of any other Abner Jones clock at just over **17 inches**, suggesting that the case that originally housed this movement was probably unlike that of any other known Abner Jones shelf clock.

differences. The assistance of a number of collectors was necessary in order to compile this information, and their contributions are greatly appreciated.[1]

We have previously reviewed the fact that similar-looking Jones shelf clock *cases* will nonetheless vary slightly in dimensions due to their hand-built nature. The same holds true for the visual appearance of Abner Jones' brass movements. For example, the shelf clock movement plates *generally* measure around 4" wide and 5¾" high, but differences appear from clock to clock. In addition, elements such as the locations of the holes for attaching the dial pillar posts to the front plates will vary. Some front plates show evidence of multiple pillar post holes where realignments were apparently necessary. While the basic gear train layouts for all of the Abner Jones movements are *similar* (i.e., all have 5-wheel time-and-strike trains), the gear counts do differ.

The analysis shows that the shift from tall to shelf clock cases resulted in significant modifications in the earlier tall clock movements, especially on the strike side. With respect to the shelf clock movements, comparisons show a great deal of uniformity, with most of the variations appearing in the escape wheel teeth counts. The escape wheel count has a direct relationship to the length of the respective pendulum, which in turn determines the necessary internal dimensions of the host case.

Of interest is the question of whether the variations in computed pendulum lengths are related to the size of the cases in which they appear (i.e., whether the movements were modified to fit in specific cases). The answer appears to be yes. For example, *Clocks 1-A* (the **Group One** timepiece) and *1-J*, another **Group One** clock but with a time-and-strike movement, both feature similar interior case dimensions, with overall heights of **approximately 26"**. Both **Group One** movement time train gear counts compute to pendulum lengths of **approximately 20"**. **Group Two** cases have the same interior dimensions as the **Group One** clocks. As noted in earlier chapters, the **Group One and Two** cases typically feature bottom case boards gouged out to allow room so that the bottom of the respective pendulum rods do not rub as the pendulum swings. In other words, these are tight fits.

The interior dimensions in the **Group Three through Eight** clock cases are significantly more accommodating than those of **Groups One and Two**. For example, the case of *Clock 3-B* offers nearly **37" of interior height**, and *Clock 4-N*, representing the Carved Scroll Top clocks, has **32" of available interior height**. The computed pendulum lengths for these later cases are concomitantly larger, as shown in **Figure 208**.

Movement Back Plate Cutouts:

The pendulums on Abner Jones' shelf clocks are *almost always* (see below) suspended from a stud off the back of the back plate. A cutout in the lower edge of the back plate serves the purpose of offering the individual greater access when removing or re-hanging the pendulum. The most common cutout form – a triangular or "A" shape – nonetheless varies from clock to clock, indicating that there was a general intent to the design but certainly no template, as shown in **Figures 209-212**.

As we have noted, Abner Jones clearly had journeymen working for him to make and assemble movements, and it is possible that individual workers preferred certain back plate cutout forms over those of other workers. We have, of course, come to expect surprises and anomalies from Abner Jones, and with respect to back plate cutout forms we do have several significant deviations from the semi-standard "A" shape or triangular form, and certainly others might exist on clocks not yet examined. One, as shown in **Figure 213**, is found on *Clock 1-F*, an early **Group One** clock with cornice top, round sides and three cabinet drawers. This form, a graduated set of large and smaller rectangles, has not, to date, been seen on any other Jones shelf clock.

Our second "deviation from the norm" is found in *Clock 1-B*, the very early **Group One** clock housing the exceptional movement #96, as extensively reviewed in **Chapter Four**.

Unlike any other Abner Jones shelf clock found to date, movement #96 in *Clock 1-B* has a circular cutout, as shown in **Figure 214**.

Bracketology:

Adapting his tall clock movement, where a suspension stud off the back plate is typical, to shelf clock use created a logistical problem for Abner Jones. Tall clock movements sit on wooden seat boards that are positioned on supports in the case such that there are generally two or more inches between the back of the movement and the back of the case, allowing tight but sufficient access to hang the pendulum. Tall clock cases may provide from 6"-8" of total (back to front) "inside" space; Jones' shelf clocks provide only around 4".

The shelf clock movements do not utilize seat boards that sit on supports as with tall clocks, but rather are secured by screws to the back board of the case. Barely adequate clearance between the back of the movement and the back of the case is provided by brackets in the form of *wood spacer strips*, which are *approximately* ¾" in depth, 1"-1½" wide and 7" long. As might be expected,

Figure 209
Back plate cutout Clock 1-B.

Figure 210
Back plate cutout Clock 3-A.

Figure 211
Back plate cutout Clock 4-A.

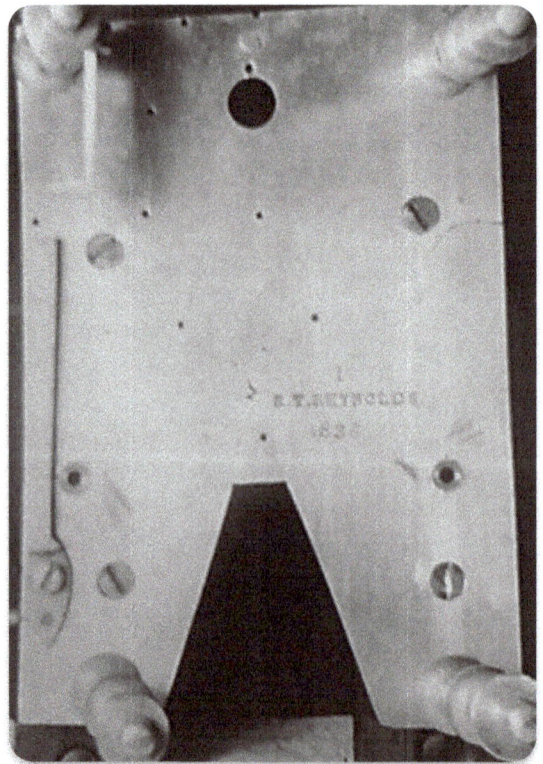

Figure 212
Back plate cutout Clock 6-A.

All Photos on Page 128 Courtesy Evan Edwards

Figures 213 & 214

Figure 213 (top): Graduated rectangles form this unusual back plate cutout on Clock 1-F, an early Group One clock with cornice top, round sides and three lower drawers.
Figure 214 (bottom): Back plate circular cutout form found (to date) only on movement #96 in Clock 1-B.

Photo Courtesy Ralph Pokluda

Photo Courtesy Tom Grimshaw

Chapter Ten • **129**

these dimensions will differ from clock to clock. Screws at the four corners of the movement back plate secure the movement to the wood spacer strips, then screws at the top and bottom of each strip secure the whole to the case. A typical movement-spacer strip assembly as found on *Clock 6-D* is shown in **Figure 215**.

Three of the screws linking the movement to the spacer strips — both top and the lower right screws — can be readily removed or re-secured to the wood strips as needed, but access to the lower left screw is blocked by the strike great wheel, making removal of the strike side spacer strip extremely difficult without totally disassembling the movement. This is a bit of a hindrance to movement repair, but more ominously *may* act to conceal movement numbers from inquisitive owners and researchers.

This possibility was uncovered when *Clock 1-A*, the Abner Jones timepiece, was first examined and the number "150" was found on the right edge of the rear of the back plate under the wood strip (*see Figure 216*).

Are there other Jones clocks where the movement number was stamped on the back plate under the wood spacer strip? Perhaps, but since numbers in this location can only be seen if the movement is removed from the case and the strips from the movement, we may simply never know.

---— *Figure 215* ---—

The typical method for securing the Abner Jones shelf clock movements to the backboard is shown, with screws at the four corners of the movement back plate linking the movement to two wood spacer strips, and then screws at the top and base of the strips securing the overall assembly to the back board of the case. The movement shown is from Clock 6-D.

Photo Courtesy Evan Edwards

Figure 216

The back plate of Clock 1-A, *the Abner Jones Timepiece, showing the movement number "150" that was concealed behind the left side (as viewed from the front of the clock) wood spacer strip.*

Are there exceptions to the use of wood spacer strips in Abner Jones' shelf clocks? Of course! To date the author has been able to identify three clocks that prove exceptions to the wood spacer strip rule by using **cast brass mounting strips riveted to the back plate**.

Our first example is the movement found in *Clock 7-D*, a late sharp cornice case with three drawers and turned columns. A picture of the movement is shown in **Figure 217**. The cast brass mounting strips riveted to the back plate of the movement can be seen emerging from the strike side of the movement. The brass strips in this instance are screwed into two extra-wide wood spacer strips. The utility of mounting the brass strips to the back of the movement can be pondered. This has the effect of allowing better access to the screws securing the movement to the wood spacer strips and thus would facilitate removing the movement from the case without having to remove the wood strips.

Additionally, this arrangement allows the wood spacer strips to more widely straddle the movement, potentially preventing any interference between the pendulum swing and the wood strips. Whether either of these factors was actually considered while making this modification is not known.

Figure 217

Photo of the movement of Clock 7-D showing the use of cast brass strips riveted to the movement back plate to secure the movement to the wood spacer strips.

Our second example reflecting the use of brass mounting strips riveted to the movement back plate is found in *Clock 4-F*, a carved scroll top case with carved columns and a mirror door, one of the special clocks we reviewed in **Chapter Six** that has a rare *one-piece dial*. The movement front and rear views are shown in **Figures 218 and 219**, respectively.

As with the movement in *Clock 7-D* above, this clock features extra-wide wood spacer strips. Due to these similar production features, it may be speculated that the movements in these two clocks, though of different case styles, were produced around the same time.

Our final, and ostensibly most interesting, movement with brass mounting strips is shown below. This loose, unnumbered movement, designated **Movement LM-1**, is a rare and, so far as currently known, "one-of-a-kind" movement for reasons other than its cast brass mounting strips, but we will examine that feature first. **Figure 220** shows the movement back plate with the riveted mounting strips and other compelling features.

Sharp observers will immediately note that the lower brass strip is not truncated, as it was on the movement in *Clocks 7-D and 4-F*, because the strip does not have to straddle any cutout in the back plate. But where did the

Figure 218

Front plate view of the movement found in Clock 4-F. The cast brass strips secured to the wooden spacer strips can be seen extending from each side of the back plate.

Figure 219

Back plate of the movement from Clock 4-F showing how the brass mounting strips are riveted into the back plate. The stud supporting the pendulum rod suspension spring is shown at the top, and the crutch wire can be seen extending out from a hole in the upper plate.

Figure 220

Rear view of the loose movement designated LM-1 showing the cast brass mounting strips riveted into the back plate. The movement has several anomalies, including the lack of a back plate cutout and, most importantly, the lack of an external suspension bracket for the pendulum rod.

Photo Courtesy Chris Tahk

cutout found in **almost all** *(except for this and one other known movement)* Abner Jones' shelf clock movements go? And perhaps most importantly, where is the suspension stud for the pendulum rod that is **always** *(except for this movement)* found on Abner Jones' shelf clock movements? Last on the "missing components" list is the crutch wire that normally protrudes through a hole in the back plate and connects the pendulum rod to the movement verge and escape wheel. **Movement LM-1** is just full of surprises.

This is indeed an important and unique movement, as the lack of a back plate cutout, and the missing exterior pendulum suspension stud and crutch wire are all due to the fact that on this movement *the suspension is hung from a stud on the back of the front plate* **between the plates**, not from the rear of the back plate. The back plate cutout is no longer needed to access the pendulum rod behind the movement, so it has been eliminated, but now the pendulum rod has to be accessed between the plates, *so the cutout appears on the front plate of the movement*, as seen in **Figure 221**.

The front plate reveals another anomaly – the lack of any holes drilled into the plate to take the inner dial feet. The one other clock with this feature, *Clock 4-A*, never had an inner dial so the movement was visible through the outer dial. So it would appear that **Movement LM-1** was similarly exposed in its original case.

Figures 222 and 223 show views of the internal stud for the pendulum rod suspension spring on the inside of the front plate. This appears to be the same type of stud used on all of the Jones' movements, but on this clock, for unknown reasons, the top and bottom sides of the round stud have been filed flat.

A view of the time-and-strike gear trains of **Movement LM-1** is shown in **Figure 224**. As shown, the crutch wire extends down from the verge arbor to intersect with the pendulum rod below. The hook at the end of the crutch wire that holds the pendulum rod has broken off as shown in the picture.

And so it is that we are once again allowed and encouraged to speculate on the motives and intentions of

Figure 221

Front plate view of Movement LM-1 showing the oval cutout in the front plate created to allow better access to the pendulum rod hung from a stud between the plates. The internal crutch wire is shown extending down within the cutout.

Photo Courtesy Chris Tahk

Figures 222 & 223

Figure 222 (left): View of the inside of the front plate of Movement LM-1 showing the internal pendulum rod suspension stud in the lower center of the plate. Figure 223 (right): A close-up showing the flat, filed surface on the bottom of the stud.

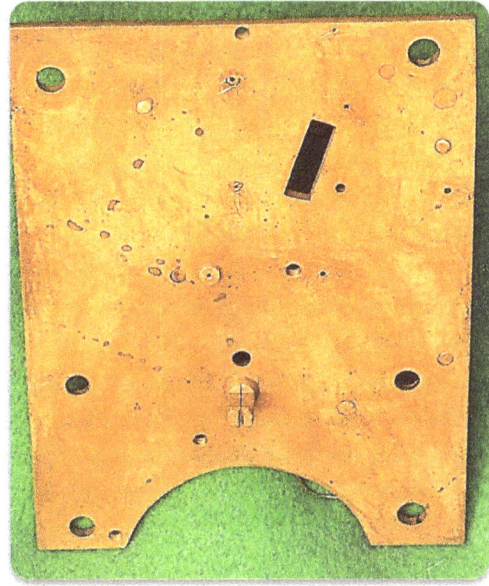 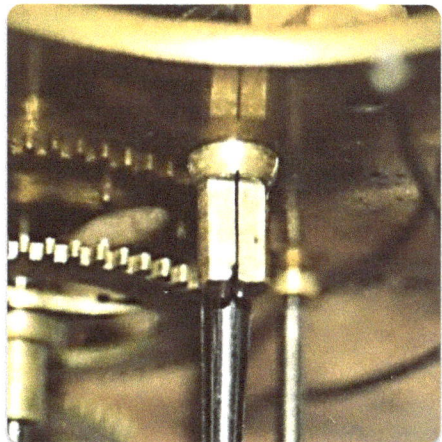

Photos Courtesy Chris Tahk

Chapter Ten • 135

Figure 224

View of Movement LM-1 *with the front plate removed revealing the time (right) and strike (left) trains and the internal crutch wire extending from the verge arbor to the bottom of the movement.*

Photo Courtesy Chris Tahk

Abner Jones. What advantages would a movement with the suspension between the plates provide and how might those advantages have been employed?

Relocating the suspension off the back plate eliminates the need for wood spacer strips behind the movement, so **Movement LM-1** would have been **screwed directly to the back board of the case from the brass mounting strips**. The advantage gained? One might be that a thinner case could be used. Thinner cases would use less material, potentially saving costs, but speculation allows consideration of the fact that a thinner, less weighty case would make it more practical to produce an **Abner Jones wall clock!**

Is this a wild notion? Well, consider, as we have previously, that Abner Jones *throughout his shelf clock production period was operating in a competitive environment.* During the mid to late 1830s, competitors Philip Smith of Marcellus, and E.W. Adams of Seneca Falls, NY, each produced wall clocks with 8-day brass movements.

Can we prove that an Abner Jones wall clock existed/exists? Unfortunately no, but consider! If there is a thin(ner), empty Abner Jones clock case stored in a

Figure 225

View from the top of Movement LM-1 *showing three plate pillar posts with drilled holes.*

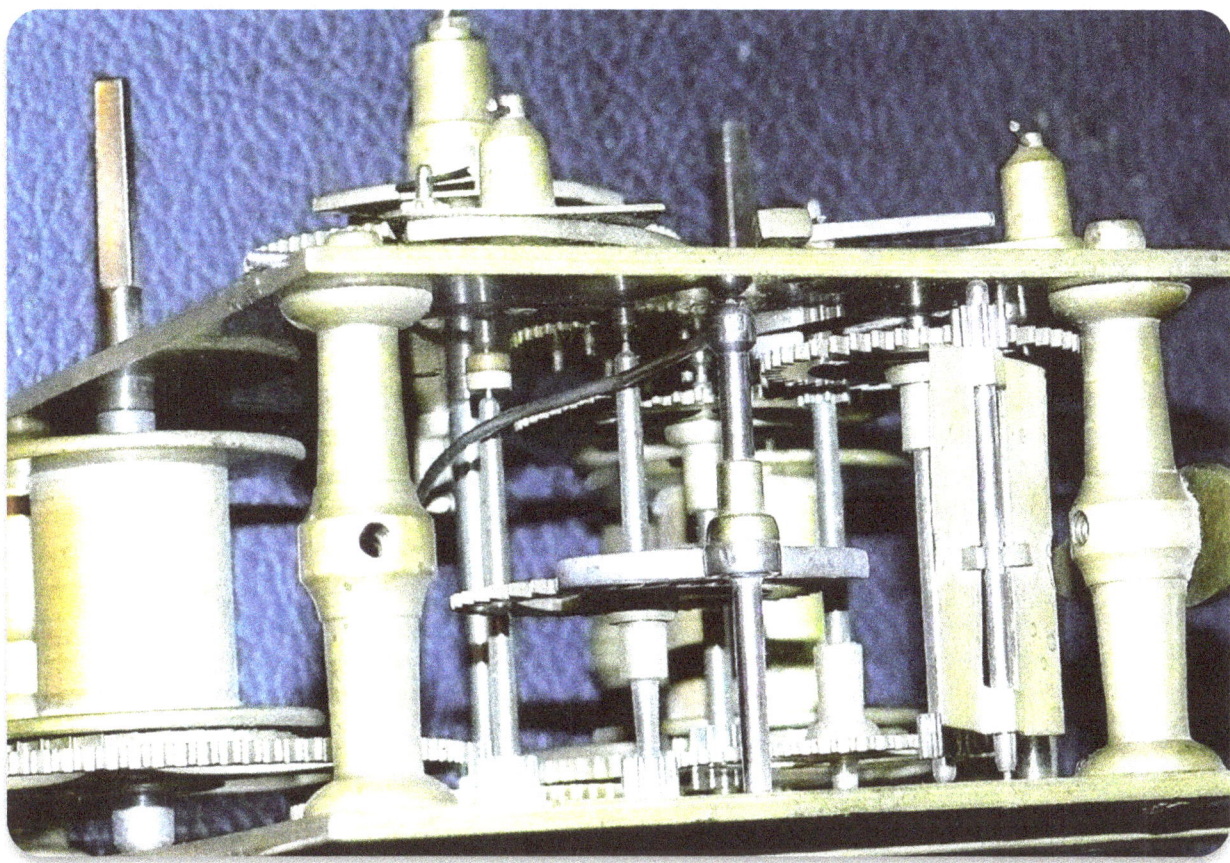

Photo Courtesy Chris Tahk

basement, attic or barn out there (maybe resembling a New Hampshire wall mirror clock?) the back board of which shows four evenly placed screw holes for the movement mounting strips **but no shadows of any wood spacer strips having ever been installed in the case**, we will have a credible candidate!

Another intriguing feature of the movement relates to the plate pillar posts. On Abner Jones' movements, the upper left pillar post is drilled in its center to accommodate a screw that holds the bell gong arm strike plate. On **Movement LM-1**, three of the plate pillar posts, the upper left, upper right and lower right, are drilled and tapped for screws. The simple explanation would be that the assembler grabbed four plate pillar posts from the parts container and three had been prepped for use on the upper strike side. **Figure 225** provides a view from the top of **Movement LM-1** showing both upper plate pillar posts as well as the lower time side post, each with drilled holes.

Alternate theories are always encouraged, of course, and one interesting fact may or may not help one postulate more effectively. A better-than-cursory review of all of the pictures available to the author showing appropriate side views of Abner Jones shelf clock movements yielded only one other movement with clearly identifiable non-upper strike side pillar posts with drilled screw holes. That is *Clock 4-A*, the only known movement **other than Movement LM-1** with a front plate that was never drilled for inner dial plate studs. There are no answers without questions.

Plate Pillar Posts

While on the topic of pillar posts we should note that at least three distinct turning forms are found on the plate pillar posts of Abner Jones shelf clocks. The most common form is shown in **Figures 226 and 227** – posts with *round center turnings that taper slightly to rounded pad feet at the plates*. *Figure 226* shows the timepiece movement from *Clock 1-A*, and **Figure 227** the movement from *Clock 6-D*.

The other plate pillar form seen, but much less frequently, has a *flattened center turning that tapers slightly to rounded feet at the plates*. An example can be seen in **Figure 228** from **Movement LM-1**.

Chapter Ten • 137

Figures 226 & 227

Figure 226 (left): Timepiece Clock 1-A exhibiting the most common plate pillar decorative form.
Figure 227 (right): Photo of the time-and-strike movement with the most common plate pillar format as found in Clock 6-D.

Figures 228 & 229

Figure 228 (left): Only a few extant Abner Jones clocks contain movements with this modified "flattened" center pillar post, as seen on loose Movement LM-1. Figure 229 (right): Only one extant clock – Clock 1-B – exhibits this highly embellished pillar post form, perhaps not surprising based on the other wonders found amid the gears and turnings in that movement.

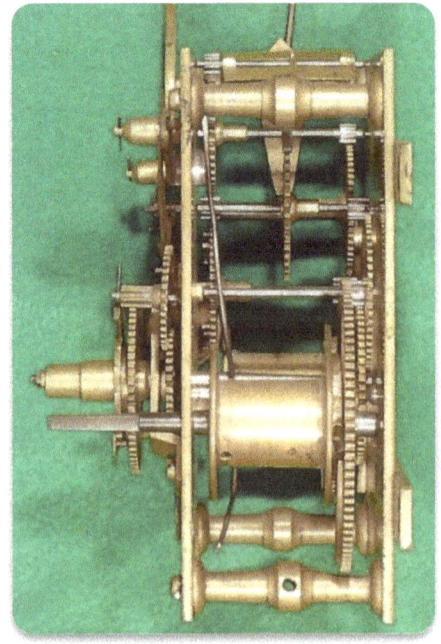

Photo Courtesy Tom Grimshaw

Photo Courtesy Chris Tahk

The final plate pillar post form seen *is a highly embellished form of the post with the rounded center, but with decorative striping*. Variations have been seen on only two clocks to date. The more elaborate form is found on *Clock 1-B*, the much-discussed extraordinary movement #96. This highly embellished post form is shown from *Clock 1-B* in **Figure 229**. *Clock 3-C*, arguably the most spectacular of all of the Abner Jones shelf clocks, also has slightly embellished plate pillar posts, which we will review at length in **Chapter 11**.

Weights

The *typical* weights found in Abner Jones' shelf clocks are rectangular, of varied dimensions and of cast iron, but there are, of course, exceptions. Granted, some of those exceptions may be replacements, but others, such as instances where well-aged cylindrical tin "cans" filled with rocks, chunks of lead, sand, etc. appear, may just as likely be original.

Two versions of cast iron weights are most often found, so those will be examined. An example of one of the "common" styles is shown in **Figure 230**. **Each weight in this set is roughly 6" in height and tapers from 2½" wide at the front top to 3¼" wide at the front base. The sides measure 2⅜" wide at the top and 2¾" wide at the base. They weigh approximately 13 lbs. each.** The weights in **Figure 230** are found in *Clock 7-D*, a late sharp cornice clock with three drawers.

The second "most common" weight style is shown in *Figure 231*. **These are nearly square and are approximately 4½" high, 3⅝" wide front and back and 3⅜" deep on each side.** The weights shown are from *Clock 3-B*, a late Full Empire case. **These weigh in at approximately 14.5 lbs. each.**

Figure 230

One of the two most common styles of cast iron weights found in Abner Jones shelf clocks. This set of original weights is found in Clock 7-D.

Photo Courtesy Evan Edwards

Figure 231

The second of the two most common styles of weights found in Abner Jones shelf clocks is shown. These weights are from Clock 3-B, a very late Full Empire case. This style is more square, and shorter and wider than the other style.

Keys

The keys found in Abner Jones' shelf clocks (and at least two of the known tall clocks) are standard and distinctive. A photo of the standard key is found in **Figure 232**. The key shaft is brass with a round turning about a third of the way down the shaft and a bulbous end where the steel crank handle is inserted. The key itself is approximately 1⅞" long and the overall length of the handle is 3" with a 1¾" long return.

Figure 232

This photo shows the standard and distinctive design of the crank keys found on Abner Jones' shelf clocks.

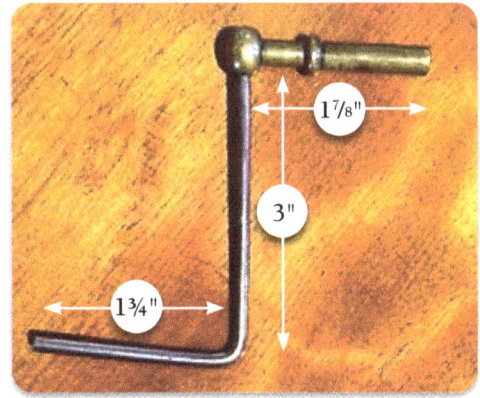

Door Closures

At last count, Abner Jones installed at least three different types of door closures on his shelf clocks. Based on observations to date, there is no apparent overall chronology, as the types overlap and intermingle.

If *Clock 1-A*, dated 1831, is indeed one of the earliest shelf clocks produced, then the same can be said of the "**Press Tab**" type of door latch that appears on this clock.

Figure 233 shows the latch from the front of the door. When the tab built into the edge of the case door is pushed downward, the hook on the arm of the latch clears a brass fitting built into the edge of the case side (*see Figure 234*). Pressure on the press tab is supplied by a spring wire attached to the back of the door (*see Figure 235*).

Figure 233
Showing the press tab found on early Clock 1-A.

Figure 234
The hook on the inside end of the tab slots into this fitting built into the edge of the case side.

Figure 235
A spring wire attached to the back of the door frame presses down on the press latch to keep the latch hook securely closed in the door.

Photo Courtesy Jeff Baker

All but two of the **Group One** clocks reviewed in **Chapter Three** utilize the **Press Tab** style of door closure. The two others utilize simple **hook-and-eye** latches, which we will review next. The press tab style did not end with early **Group One** clocks, however. They appear on several later models with modified cast brass latch tabs, as shown in **Figure 236**, which shows the press tab on *Clock 6-C*, a medium-sized sharp cornice and carved column case containing movement #50.

Figure 236
Later versions of the press tab type of door latch used a modified cast brass tab.

Photo Courtesy Jeff Baker

Simple hook-and-eye latches appear on two of the **Group One** cases, *all* of the **Group Two** cases, and a few of the very late Abner Jones shelf clocks.

On some clocks the hook is attached to the side of the case and the eye to the door, and others have the hook on the door and the eye on the case as shown in **Figure 237** from *Clock 3-B*, a late large Full Empire case.

Figure 237
This hook-and-eye type closure was used by Abner Jones on a wide variety of cases both early and late.

The third type of door closure used on Abner's shelf clock cases *and the most common based on surviving clocks*, incorporates a **push-button** release built into the side of the case. With this closure, a brass button protrudes from the left side of the case. This button is riveted within the case to a strip of spring steel that supplies pressure to the button as well as forming a catch hook for the latch built into the door edge. When the button is pushed in, the latch is released, allowing the door to be opened. A **push-button** closure is shown in *Figure 238*, including the button extending out of the side of the case, the hook end of the strip of spring steel attached to the inside of the case, and the latch attached to the back of the door. This closure is found on *Clock 4-L*, a Carved Scroll Top case with carved columns and mirror door. *Figure 239* shows in detail the spring steel strip inside the case to which the brass button is riveted, as found in *Clock 6-A*, a late, large sharp cornice and carved column clock.

Push-button closures are found on *all* of the **Group Four** Scroll Top clocks and *all* of the **Group Five** clocks seen to date, and *nearly all* of the **Group Six** clocks.

Figures 238 & 239

Figure 238 (top): Showing the push-button and door latch from Clock 4-L.
Figure 239 (bottom): Showing the spring steel strip from Clock 6-A.

Drawer Pulls

The inclusion of cabinet sections with drawers on his shelf clock cases is synonymous with Abner Jones, his calling card if you will, although by count most of his cases did not have this feature. Cabinets with drawers are furniture elements. Pulls are functional but decorative features on those drawers, selected to appeal to customers, and as such the different types of pulls used deserve review.

In general, a variety of glass drawer pulls appeared on Jones' shelf clocks, and they did change from opaque and white to clear glass over time. Pulls on lower, full drawers tend to be slightly larger than the pulls on the upper drawers (1" diameter to ¾", for example), but on some clocks the pulls are the same on all drawers. *Figures 240 – 245* present the range of glass drawer pull options while noting the clocks they appear on.

Figures 240 – 245

Figure 240 (top left): Opaque glass pull, Clock 1-G. *Figure 241 (top center): Pulls from* Clock 2-C.
Figure 242 (top right): Pulls from Clock 2-A. *Figure 243 (bottom left): Clear glass pull from* Clock 3-A.
Figure 244 (bottom center): Pulls from Clock 7-B. *Figure 245 (bottom right): Clear glass pulls from* Clock 8-A.

Door Pulls

Abner Jones clocks with drawers almost never have *door* pulls. Clocks without drawers almost always do. Few have glass door pulls; almost all door pulls are of brass. *Figures 246 – 251* present the range of door pull options while noting the clocks they appear on.

Hands

All of the various sets of hands that appear on Abner Jones shelf clocks share one unique feature — all have minute and hour hands of the same length. There were at least three styles used by Jones prior to adopting his most common form, and all appeared on the earliest **Group One** clocks. They are shown, in apparent chronological order, in *Figures 252 through 255*.

The most iconic, and common, type is that of brass, where the hour hand has an open heart-shaped pointer, and a minute hand with a solid spade pointer, as shown in *Figure 255*.

Pendulum Bobs

Several styles of bobs are found on Abner Jones shelf clocks without discernable chronology. Examples are shown in *Figures 256 through 259*.

Shelf Clocks by the Numbers

The *number* of shelf clocks made by Abner Jones has always been of interest to collectors, an interest fueled by the legend that "*Abner Jones only made 100 clocks.*" One of the tasks of this work has always been to examine that legend and distinguish myth from reality. Based on this study of the extant Abner Jones shelf clocks, we can provide some answers.

At the time of this publication, **a total of *61* surviving Abner Jones shelf clocks (including two loose movements) have been documented.** This total includes three clocks cataloged by Evan Edwards (EAE #28, #29 and #39 – see Appendix I) that could not be located by the author.

Figures 246 – 251

Figure 246 (top left): Door pull from Clock 4-J. Figure 247 (top center): Door pull from Clock 4-B. Figure 248 (top right): Door pull from Clock 5-A. Figure 249 (bottom left): Door pull from Clock 6-A. Figure 250 (bottom center): Door pull from Clock 6-D. Figure 251 (bottom right): Door pull from Clock 7-B.

  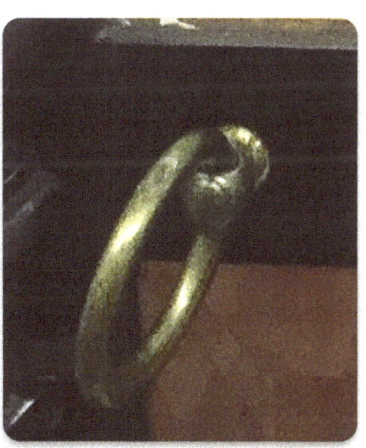

Figure 252
The earliest known hands utilized by Jones on a shelf clock were this set – cut down steel Abner Jones tall clock hands – as found on Clock 1-A.

Figure 253
Only one clock – Clock 1-B – utilizes the very attractive cut-steel hand set, with an open heart shape on the hour hand and open half-moon on the minute hand.

Figure 254
The majority of the Group One time-and-strike Jones clocks featured this style of cut-steel hands.

Figure 255
The cast brass hands so synonymous with Abner Jones are found on the vast majority of his clocks.

Figures 256 – 259

Figure 256 (top): Bob front and back from Clock 1-A. Figure 257 (second from top): Bob front and back found on Clock 2-A. Figure 258 (third from top): Bob front and back from Clock 2-B. Figure 259 (bottom): Bob front and back found on late Clock 6-B

Of these 61 clocks or loose movements, 24, or approximately 40%, have or are movements with stamped numbers or dates, or both.

Within this subgroup of 24 inscribed movements, the lowest identified stamped number is "**2**" and the highest number found to date on a time-and-strike movement is "**96**". Only the one extant timepiece movement is numbered higher, at "**150**". The earliest inscribed year on any movement is "**1831**" (on the abovementioned timepiece movement). One time-and-strike movement is dated "**1832**" and also carries the movement number "**6**". Two movements carry the stamped dates "**1835**". No later *dated* movements have been recorded.

Figure 260 details the total number of clocks per case type Group and the number of clocks within each group with numbered or dated movements. As noted above, three of the clocks documented by Evan Edwards cannot be located, and one numbered movement, **#71**, and the unique movement we designated **LM-1** lack cases, so 56 individual clocks are detailed below. There is at least one clock with a numbered or dated movement in each group. Half or fewer of the clocks in each group are numbered or dated, with the exception of Group Six, the ***Sharp Cornice Top Cases Without Drawers***, wherein, remarkably, seven of the nine extant examples are numbered, with a range between #50 and #95.

The numbers tell us that *we cannot prove that Abner Jones made more than 100 shelf clocks*. At the same time, our tally of extant clocks appears to belie that notion. Over the years, researchers have often addressed the question of how many of the hundreds of thousands (millions?) of shelf clocks made by American producers after 1800 have survived to the present. The percentage is open to speculation, but by any account it would be very small.[2]

If Abner Jones produced, according to legend, 100 or fewer clocks, the apparent documented survival rate would be at least 60%. In comparison with other American makers could this survival rate be possible?

Reason would suggest the answer "*Almost certainly not…,*" but let's try to describe a scenario where the numbers might work. Consider the fact that these are, by all *appearances*, very unusual and unique (in many ways) clocks. Consider that the size of the Abner Jones shelf clocks makes them impossible to ignore, and they are so monumental that even the most thoughtless and uneducated of owners might think twice before disposing of them.

These clocks were very expensive and *high-value* commodities when bought (see price estimates below), and have generally continued to be such in comparison to other American shelf clocks. Lastly, most of these clocks were originally sold in East or West Bloomfield, Ontario County, and neighboring counties. Because they were identified and respected as a local product, they were often seen as significant regional and family heirlooms. As our ***Back Stories*** have revealed, many of these clocks were so valued that they remained with the same families over many generations, giving them added protection from the vagaries of fashion and trends regarding the value of historic artifacts.

So is it possible that the Abner Jones *numbers* are to be believed? Did he make 100 or fewer clocks, and *might* 60% of the shelf clocks he made still exist? Our research shows that the answer, as unlikely as it may seem, could be yes.

Figure 260

Extant Abner Jones Shelf Clocks with Movement Numbers & Dates by Case Type

CASE TYPE	# EXTANT	# WITH NUMBERED OR DATED MOVEMENTS	RANGE
Group 1	10	5	1831, 1832; #2, 3, 6, 96; 150
Group 2	8	1	#4
Group 3	3	1	1835
Group 4	14	5	1835; #49, 59, 76, 77
Group 5	5	1	#48
Group 6	9	7	#50, 56, 64, 87, 90, 91, 95
Group 7	4	2	#57, 65
Group 8	3	1	#88

Note: Loose movement #71 is not listed.

At What Cost?

Producers of goods have a fundamental choice as to the market in which they wish to engage and the buyers they hope to attract. The maker might decide to aim for the mass market by aggressively reducing production costs with a plan to offset smaller profit margins with sales volume, or, alternatively, might attempt to profit by spending more on the product to appeal to wealthier buyers willing to pay more for the cachet that goes with rarity and exclusivity. With the former option precluded by the high-volume Connecticut producers, Jones chose the latter.

So what might an Abner Jones shelf clock have cost the buyer in the 1830-1840 period? A great question, but answers are, alas, hard to come by. None of the documentation associated with the Jones shelf clocks known to the author mentions original prices, a fact typical of all of the other upstate New York 8-day brass shelf clockmakers except, fortunately, one. We do have cost information for the high-end clocks made by E. (Elmer) W. Adams of Seneca Falls in the 1836-37 period, courtesy of an original account book of clock peddler Franklin M. Merrills (aka *Merrells*), a copy of which was found in the microfilm archives of the National Association of Watch & Clock Collectors by the late researcher Ward Francillon.[3]

In the fall and winter of 1836-37, Adams hired Merrills, of East Haddam, CT, to peddle clocks for him in western New York.[4] Merrills and four other peddlers traveled largely by sleigh in the winter months, which was common in the period as it was actually much easier to traverse the countryside in the winter than on unimproved or impassable roads in other seasons.

From that account book, we can document that E.W. Adams sold his wooden works shelf clocks for $5 and $7 each, and 8-day brass, time-and-strike movement clocks for $15 to $30, depending upon case styles. Adams' premier "*No. 1 Brass*" product was his full-column and cornice model, as shown in **Figure 261**. These sold in 1836-37 for $25, or $30 if the buyer preferred the clock with paw feet.[5]

Figure 261

E.W. Adams' premier 8-day brass movement shelf clock was this full-column and cornice model with paw feet.

One additional source of information is available, again related to E.W. Adams. After his declaration of bankruptcy in October, 1837, Adams' factory was seized and secured for his creditors by the local Sheriff. As detailed in a local newspaper account, one night thereafter, Adams and cohorts broke into the factory and cleared out the contents onto canal boats and, as the reporter noted, "*took Horace Greeley's advice and went west.*" The Sheriff took up the chase, but was unable to catch Adams before he cleared Buffalo into Lake Erie. Adams secured a sales location at Chillicothe, OH, where he sold his remaining inventory in early 1838.[6] Due to a remarkable surviving document, we now know that Adams sold his brass clocks in Ohio "from $35 to $60."[7]

What can be inferred, then, from the scant, but informative, data that we have is that the market for high-end 8-day brass movement shelf clocks made in upstate New York likely started in the range of $25 per clock, and perhaps ranged up to $50 or more. For discussion purposes, if we assume that Abner Jones' clocks were at the high end of the comparative scale, what might the price of, say, $45 in 1840 translate into 2020 dollars?

According to a study by Oregon State University professor Robert Sahr of the Bureau of Labor Statistics' *Consumer Price Index* (CPI) for the period 1840 to 2020, the sum of $45 in 1840 was the rough equivalent of over $1,300 in 2020.[8]

See Appendices A through H to see a listing of each extant Abner Jones shelf clock by Group and characteristics, and see Appendix J to see a complete listing of every numbered and dated Abner Jones shelf clock.

---

[1] The author is especially appreciative of the contributions of Frederick (Chris) Tahk, who reviewed the gear count data and computed the estimated pendulum lengths. It is with supreme sadness that the author must note that Chris, a true scholar and excellent researcher, passed away in November, 2020 during final preparation of this book. In addition to the author, several great contributors provided individual movement data, including Tom Grimshaw, Ben Orszulak and the late Charles Parsons.

[2] Communication with Chris Bailey.

[3] NAWCC Research Library, Columbia, PA. Microfilm Box 3/18; Roll E.

[4] Franklin Merrills [Merrells] is most famous for his involvement with Chauncey Jerome in the 1840s. Jerome claimed Merrills had defrauded him of $40,000 worth of clocks. In Jerome's words, "*This young man was well brought up, but bad company ruined him and others with him.*" (From Jeromes' *History of the American Clock Business for the Past Sixty Years, and Life of Chauncey Jerome*, F.C. Dayton, New Haven, CT, 1860.)

[5] Oechsle, G. Russell and Boyce, Helen. *An Empire in Time: Clocks and Clock Makers of Upstate New York*, National Association of Watch & Clock Collectors, Inc., Columbia, PA, 2003, p. 83.

[6] Ibid. p. 84.

[7] *Letter from David Grigg of Waterford, NY, to his brother Daniel Chillicothe, OH, dated April 15, 1838.* Collection of Ruth Hirshfield.

[8] www.officialdata.org/us/inflation/1840?amount=45.

CHAPTER ELEVEN

Full Empire Clocks and Abner's Opus

Chapter Eleven will detail three clocks described as Group Three, all "Full Empire" models. Though the cases of each surely exhibit characteristic Empire furniture influences, these clocks are somewhat arbitrarily grouped together for several reasons. First, their overall compositions are different from any of the other cases found to date; they do share *some* case characteristics, such as their prominent half columns; two of the three appear to be *very late clocks – perhaps two of the last*; and most specifically, they each feature dials unlike those found on any other Abner Jones shelf clocks.

Our first clock was reviewed in **Chapter Five** as *Clock 3-A*. As a reminder, a photo of the clock is shown as ***Figure 262***. As noted, this is a very large case. At approximately 53" in height including feet, it is unique in form among the extant Abner Jones shelf clocks.

Figure 262

Clock 3-A, with the date 1835 and inscription on the back plate of "G.W. Berry" and the date 1835.

Photo Courtesy Evan Edwards

Despite the 1835 dating, the four-drawer base on *Clock 3-A* is very reminiscent of the **Group Eight** cases with four drawers. One clock in the latter group has a movement numbered #88, which would indicate a late production, so *Clock 3-A* may have been the example on which some elements of those later models were based.

Most interesting, especially with respect to the apparent 1835 production date of this clock, is the fact that it incorporates a dial unlike any seen prior to, or indeed, later in Jones' production. This is still a two-piece dial with a "standard" inner dial, but with an outer dial with a chapter ring that is significantly smaller in size than any other known two-piece Abner Jones dial. In addition, it is the least embellished/decorated of any known Jones dial. As shown in **Figure 263**, the Roman numerals are surrounded by a ribbon-like gold edging, but otherwise, the spandrels are spare – mere gilt outlines.

The descriptive terms "monumental" and "remarkable" come to mind, and *Clocks 3-B and 3-C* surely fit that bill as well.

The second clock in the group is *Clock 3-B*. As shown in F**igure 264**, this is a very large, Full Empire case with no drawers. The case measures **43⅝" tall; 23¼" wide and 9¼" deep at the base; 25⅞" wide and 10⅜" deep at the cornice top; and 20" wide and 7⅞" deep in the central case**. The case has a sharp cornice top but a base section resembling, in reverse, the sloped molding found on the top of the **Group Five** clocks. The entire case, including the half columns, is veneered in figured mahogany. The lower door panel is a mirror. The edge molding just below the cornice, the thin blocks above each column, the edge molding on both doors and a molding line along the bottom of the main case are ebonized.

The movement of *Clock 3-B* is not numbered. The door is secured with a hook-and-eye type closure.

The most unusual feature of *Clock 3-B*, actually unique among all known Jones shelf clocks, is its dial and its decorative spandrel treatment. This clock has a ***round, one-piece dial***, so typical of clocks by other makers in this period that it would only be worthy of mention for its singularity in the context of Abner Jones. The round white dial, now restored as original with Roman numerals, measures 8⅞" in diameter, and has three dial feet that are secured to the front plate of the movement in the same

Figure 263

The unique and minimally-decorated dial found on Clock 3-A.
While it is a two-piece dial, the outer dial is smaller than any other found on a Jones shelf clock.

Photo Courtesy the Steele Family

Figure 264

Clock 3-B is a Full Empire case in mahogany veneer and features the only known Jones clock with a single, round zinc dial with decorative spandrels reverse painted on the dial glass.

manner as the inner dials on other Jones shelf clocks. A picture of the single dial of *Clock 3-B* is shown in **Figure 265**, and the back of the dial in **Figure 266**.

It is interesting to note that this clock, with a "normal" dial format, would lend itself to "normal" hands, with minute hands lengthened to reach the dial edge, and a shorter hour hand. Nonetheless, the standard Abner Jones brass hands of equal length were installed.

Unlike any other Jones shelf clock examined so far, the decorative spandrels on *Clock 3-B* are **reverse painted on the upper dial glass**, as shown in **Figure 267**, with a close-up of the spandrel decorations in **Figure 268**.

Figures 265 & 266

Figure 265 (top): The restored, one-piece zinc dial from Clock 3-B.
Figure 266 (bottom): Back of the dial plate from Clock 3-B *showing the three dial feet that secure the dial to the movement.*

152 • *Without Equal: The Clocks of Abner Jones of Bloomfield, New York*

Figure 267

Clock 3-B has a single round dial and reverse painted spandrels on the upper glass – unique among known Abner Jones shelf clocks.

Figure 268

A close-up view of the decorative reverse painted spandrels on glass surrounding the one-piece dial of Clock 3-B.

Chapter Eleven • 153

The floral decorations in the spandrels are reminiscent of the dials of the earliest **Group One** clocks and in some respects the simplified floral dials of the **Group Eight** clocks, but stylistically they are distinct.

There is one other clock with the exact same dial decorations though presented in a different format. It is wonderfully fitting that what appears by design and features to be the latest production Abner Jones shelf clock to have survived (at least into the 20th century) is also the most spectacular. This clock, *Clock 3-C*, is shown in **Figure 270**.

Our knowledge of this spectacular clock comes solely from a set of black and white photos *(tinted in our illustrations to somewhat better impart the beauty of the piece)*, part of the **Buel-Barr Study**, the mid-1930s work of noted horological researcher Lockwood Barr and photographer Carlton Buel. Edward and Dudley Ingraham, principals of the E. Ingraham Clock Company of Bristol, CT, provided the funds to support the production of the *Study*, which was originally planned to be published. That never happened, and at least three copies were reportedly produced, one of which is in the collection of the American Clock & Watch Museum at Bristol, CT.[1] The preface of the work was a manuscript entitled *History of Clockmaking in Bristol, Connecticut*. Four volumes of photographs with descriptions completed each copy of the *Study*, including the pictures shown here of *Clock 3-C*. The search for this clock continues.[2]

Below is a copy of the description (**Figure 269**) that accompanied the photo shown in **Figure 270**. As noted, the authors could not identify the maker of the clock, but stated that the movement was "*quite unique in several respects.*" Four other photos were included, and each will be examined below.[3]

Figure 269
Document Courtesy Buel-Barr Study.

8-Day Brass Movement for Shelf Clock

(Maker Unknown)

This 8-Day brass movement for a shelf clock is quite unique in several respects. It is the only such movement known. It is a replica in miniature of the 8-Day brass movement for tall clocks made circa 1775-1800. The strike train is actuated by a Rack & Snail mechanism, the bell being mounted above and on the front plate. The Escape Wheel with Verge above, is between the plates as in the case of the tall clock. The crutch wire extends through an opening in the back plate actuating the pendulum which is hung from a post on the back plate. The weights are compounded, falling about 30 inches and the pendulum is circa 17 1/2 inches.

Figure 270

This is the only known picture of Abner Jones Clock 3-C, perhaps Jones' ultimate clock; current whereabouts are unknown.

Photo Courtesy Buel-Barr Study

A comparison between *Clock 3-B* and the photographs of the case of *Clock 3-C* reveals that the **case bases**, consisting of the reverse sloping molding and lower door structures, appear to be similar on both clocks. The same holds for the turned **column bases**. The round half columns on *Clock 3-B* measure 32¾" in height. By rough reckoning, the columns on *Clock 3-C* appear to be approximately 2" taller than those on *Clock 3-B*, and feature two sectional turnings not seen on *Clock 3-B*. The turned upper column caps differ slightly.

Top treatments differ considerably, as the upper box section at the top of *Clock 3-B* is set between two flat moldings under a thin, round edge molding under a *sharp* cornice top measuring 4" in height. *Clock 3-C* has a top unlike any other found on a known Jones shelf clock. The box section of perhaps 2" in height angles out from the thin, flat base molding. This is capped by an approximately 1" round molding, then another thin flat molding under a sloped cornice top. The overall height of the cornice top appears to be approximately 5½"-6". The thin ebonized trim molding seen on *Clock 3-B* is utilized in the same way on *Clock 3-C*. Overall, if *Clock 3-B* measures 43⅝", *Clock 3-C* may total approximately 48"-50" in height.

The additional height of *Clock 3-C* is reflected in the taller upper door glass, which acts as the tableau for the supreme artistry of Abner Jones. As seen in **Figure 271**, the elongated glass door tablet employs a reverse-painted surround with the same colorful (if we could see them) decorations as found on the spandrels of *Clock 3-B*. Within the decorative framing is what appears to be a 6" lower, round, transparent dial opening with reverse-painted Roman numerals over a highly polished presentation movement, and an upper round opening with reverse-painted floral decorations in the center over a polished brass bell. The bell is mounted on a circular support bracket secured from the top of the front plate of the movement. The gong hammer is not round, as with every other known Abner Jones movement, but a flattened disc. The door pull appears to be clear glass – a smaller version of the bulbous glass drawer pulls seen on the **Group Eight** clocks.

While the case is spectacular, the movement within the case is truly a singular work of art. Aspects of this special movement will be revealed in *Figures 272 – 274*.

Figure 272 (see page 158) shows the front view of the movement of *Clock 3-C*. Interesting features appear wherever one looks. The lower front plate has a half-moon cutout, and the back plate is solid, with no cutout.

Remarkably, the front plate contains three **"exclamation mark" cutouts** – two flanking the center arbor and motion work, and the third angled right to left below the escape wheel pivot. Without equal, indeed.

Also of significant interest is the statement included within the *Buel-Barr Study's* description of this movement (see page 154) that *"the pendulum is circa 17 1/2 inches."* As noted in the comparison of Abner Jones movement gear counts shown in **Figure 208** (see page 126), this pendulum length is unusual, and as such may mean that the time side gear counts for *Clock 3-C* match those found on the (so far) unique movement *LM-1*.

The bell is secured from a circular bracket, the arms of which are screwed into the upper edge of the front plate.

Figure 273 (see page 159) presents a view of the time side of the movement. This aspect reveals that the bell bracket extends perhaps 1½" out from the front plate and that the wood spacer strips on this clock are unusually long and not straight, but with centers wider than the ends. The plate pillar posts have added incised rings, and unlike any other observed Abner Jones movement, the front plate is secured to the plate pillar posts by screws rather than with pins. The movement does not appear to be numbered.

Figure 274 (see page 159) shows the strike side view of the movement. All of the standard Abner Jones strike side components are evident.

For a detailed comparison of all of the Group Three clocks, see Appendix C.

---

[1] Personal communication with Chris Bailey.

[2] *Bulletin of the National Association of Watch and Clock Collectors.* Vol. III, No.2, Whole #22, p. 374.

[3] Copies of the original photos were provided to the author in 2001 by the late Ward Francillon. Ward had obtained a partial copy of the *Buel-Barr Study* from Ed Burt who, he had been told, secured the copy from Albert Partridge, Secretary of the "Old Clock Club of Boston" and a contemporary of the Ingrahams.

Figure 271

The unusual and unique upper door of Clock 3-C. Within the decorative floral reverse-painted frame are two circular openings revealing the movement and the bell behind a transparent dial.

Photo Courtesy Buel-Barr Study

Chapter Eleven • 157

Figure 272
The front plate of Clock 3-C reveals an Abner Jones exercise in horological serendipity.

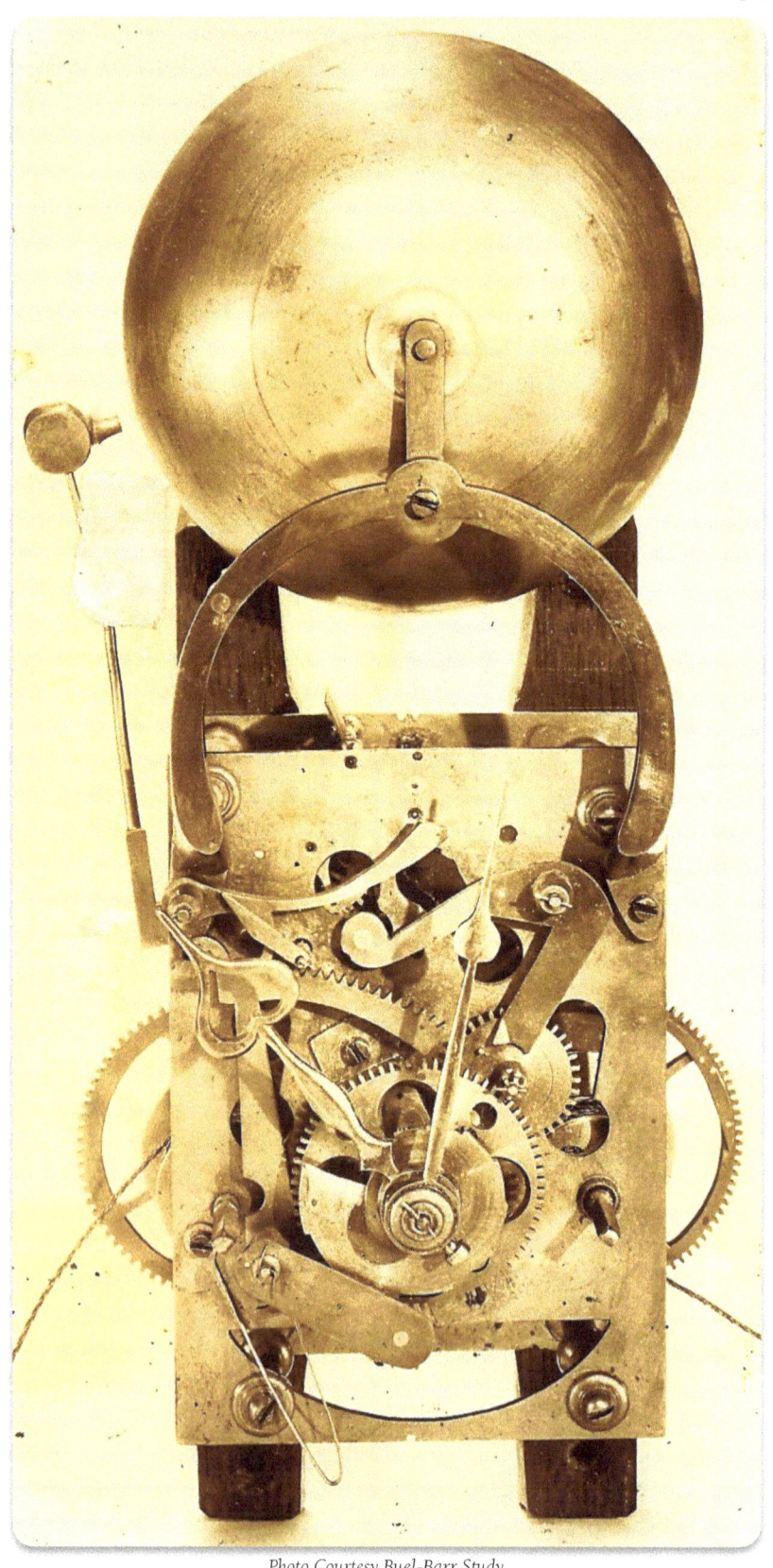

Photo Courtesy Buel-Barr Study

Figures 273 & 274

Figure 273 (left): Time side view of the movement of Clock 3-C.
Figure 274 (right): Strike side view of the movement of Clock 3-C.

Photos Courtesy Buel-Barr Study

CHAPTER TWELVE

The Time at Bloomfield Comes to an End

Abner Jones' career at West Bloomfield ended in bankruptcy in early 1841, and his production of clocks quite likely ceased sometime in the year prior. Jones and his fellow upstate New York 8-day brass shelf clockmakers had, in fact, been facing an uphill battle for some time in their attempt to remain competitive. The threats came not just in the form of high-volume Connecticut makers and their ubiquitous peddlers, but with the effects of the *Panic of 1837*, a nationwide economic crisis brought on by rampant land speculation and the collapse of the American banking system following President Andrew Jackson's failure to renew the charter of the central Second Bank of the United States. Banks failed, money became scarce, and businesses large and small, lacking credit and unable to collect on their outstanding accounts, went bankrupt overnight. The crisis was to last into 1843.[1]

Of Jones' upstate New York competitors, most, including *Hotchkiss & Benedict* at Auburn (1836), *E.W. Adams* at Seneca Falls (1837), and *Jared Arnold, Jr.* at Amber (1838), had already succumbed by 1841. Only Philip Smith at Marcellus was able to hold on until early 1842.[2]

Perhaps as a prelude to the ultimate bankruptcy, Abner and Sabra did act to pay off the $1,500 mortgage given by Evan Johns for their East Bloomfield farm purchase in 1832. The discharge was filed on April 2, 1840.[3] At that point, they remained responsible for the $1,700 mortgage loan from Charles Webb, from whom they had purchased their West Bloomfield property in 1835. One can imagine the difficulties as the clock demand dried up; individuals who may have owed Jones money could not pay, and Jones, in turn, was not able to pay his creditors.

At some point, likely in late 1840, Charles Webb of West Bloomfield filed suit in the Court of Chancery, State of New York, Ontario County for the overdue payment of Abner and Sabra's $1,700 mortgage. On May 3, 1841, at public auction on the steps of the Ontario County Courthouse, Canandaigua, NY, Webb was the high bidder at $800 for the 28-acre parcel he had sold to Abner and Sabra Jones in 1835. Interestingly, the complaint listed three additional individuals as defendants in the suit — West Bloomfield merchants and blacksmiths William and David Pilsbury (alternately spelled Pillsbury), and one Thomas Patterson, for whom no records could be identified by the author. It would appear that the listing of these three would indicate a business relationship as investors or partners in Jones' clock or foundry operations. Unfortunately, no other information has been found to clarify this relationship.[4]

Charles Webb held onto his returned property for only a few weeks. On May 31, 1841, he sold the former Jones 28-acre parcel to James H. Hall for $1,500, allowing him to recoup at least some of his losses.[5] Joseph Hall took over the Jones residence, and the foundry and clock factory building was converted into a brewery, carriage factory and blacksmith shop, as shown in **Figure 275**.

Figure 275

A portion of the 1859 Map of Ontario County showing the former Jones property at West Bloomfield then occupied by James H. Hall (underlining added).

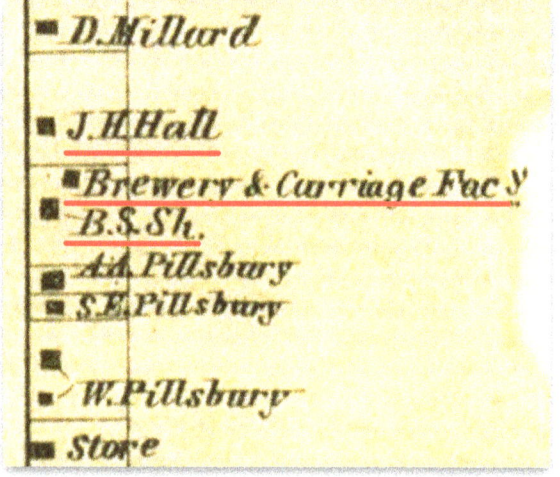

After the bankruptcy, Abner, Sabra and their children Almira (b. 1822), William (b. 1824), Oliver (b. 1825) and Charles H. (b. 1832) moved to Avon, Livingston County, NY, located approximately 15 miles due west of West Bloomfield on the Turnpike Road, now U.S. Route 20. At Avon, Abner and family took up residence, apparently as renters, on Prospect Street in the center of the village just a block off the public square. In 1842, Sabra gave birth to a daughter, Alice A. Jones, but Sabra died soon thereafter, apparently due to complications from the birth.[6]

The *1850 Census for Avon, Livingston County, NY,* lists 58-year-old Abner as employed as a brass founder, as was his son William, age 26. Almira, age 28, and Alice, age 8, were also in the household at that time.[7] Son Charles, age 18, was identified as a laborer living in the household of saddler John T. Hall, and son Oliver, age 25, was listed as a laborer working on the farm of William E. Hall.[8]

It appears that the family rented the Prospect Street property until April 1, 1854, when the house and lot were purchased from Catherine McHume under the names of Abner's son Oliver and his wife, Sarah.[9] The *1858 Map of Ontario County* (*see Figure 276*) shows the house lot in the village of Avon under the name "A. Jones."[10]

At the time of the *1855 Census*, all of the children but Charles were living with Abner at his residence. Abner was still listed as a brass founder, but now both William and Oliver were self-employed as jewelers.[11] Their shop, as shown on the 1852 Rae & Otley *Map of Livingston County, NY*, was located on Main Street just a block east of the Village Green (*see Figure 277*).[12]

By 1860, Abner, now 68 and listed in the *Census* under his old title of *"Clockmaker,"* was living in the village of Avon with his son Oliver, *Jeweler*, age 35, Oliver's wife, Sarah (H. Young), age 25, son William, *Jeweler*, age 37, daughter Almira, age 36, and Burton H. Hickox, a *"Harness Maker,"* age 27, likely a nephew of Abner's late wife, Sabra (Hickcox).[13]

The family appears to have remained largely intact in the Prospect Street home (*see Figure 278* for a view of the home at this location today) through the decade.

Burton Hickcox had moved on by 1870, but all of the other family members from 1860 remained, with the addition of Abner's son Charles, now returned to the household, and Oliver's wife Sarah's mother, Mary Young, age 67. Inexplicably Abner, age 68, is listed in the *1870 Census* as a "laborer."[14]

The *1870 Census* listing is curious, but perhaps telling. As reported in the July 13, 1876 *Livingston County Herald*, Abner Jones died on July 12th, 1876 at the age of 86. The article noted that "**during the latter days of his life his mind became somewhat impaired,**" and that his family was compelled to place him into the County Alms [or Poor] House on July 2nd. Alms House records stated that when he arrived Jones "**suffered from insanity or dementia,**" and predicted that he would "**not live over a month. He was a Clockmaker.**" Abner Jones was buried in the Avon cemetery, a short distance from his village home.[15]

Unfortunately, attempts to track the lives of Abner's children and any possible descendants met with frustration and contemplation. The last record found for Abner's oldest son, William W. Jones, born in 1824, is a listing in the *1865 Census* where he is noted as a "Jeweller" living in the Avon residence with Abner and family. He did not marry, and his date of death remains uncertain.[16]

Son Oliver C. Jones, born in 1825, married wife Sarah between 1855 and 1860. They had no children. Oliver was listed in later *Census* records as a jeweler. He and Sarah sold the Prospect Street, Avon house after Abner's death on September 18, 1877[17] and relocated to a home on East Main Street in the village. Oliver died on July 12, 1903 and is buried at Avon, NY.[18]

Son Charles Henry Jones, born in 1832 at East Bloomfield, was listed in the *1850 Census* as a "Saddler."

Figures 276 & 277

Figure 275 (left): A portion of the 1858 Map of Livingston Co. New York *showing the location of the village of Avon Jones family residence. Figure 276 (right): Red arrow indicates the Village Green, Avon, and Green arrow shows the location of the jewelry store of William and Oliver Jones, ca. 1852.*

Figures 278
The Prospect Street, village of Avon location of the Abner Jones home as it appears today.

He enlisted in the U.S. Army in 1862 and was discharged from service at the conclusion of the Civil War in 1865. He is listed in the *1870 Census* records as an unmarried harness maker living at Lima, Livingston County, NY.[19] Charles was married between 1870 and 1875 to Adaline M. Graham of Avon, widow of Patrick Graham. There is no evidence that Charles and Adaline ever had children. Charles died on July 2, 1877 at Royalton, Niagara County, NY, where he was a harness maker.[20]

The last record found for daughter Alice A. Jones, born in 1842, is her listing in the *1855 Census*, at age 13, when she lived in the Avon household. There is no indication that she ever married. Cemetery records state that she is buried at Avon, date of death uncertain.[21]

Daughter Almira H. Jones, born in 1822, is listed in a series of *Census* enumerations as unmarried, living at the Avon home with Abner and her brothers through 1860. Between 1860 and 1870, she married her distant cousin John H. Jones, son of Richard Jones, her father's nephew and one-time partner in the foundry and clock making trade at East Bloomfield. In 1870, John, age 43, and Almira, age 39, were living on their farm at Geneseo, Livingston County with Lucy Jones, John's mother.[22]

Almira and John did not have any children. Almira died on April 15, 1888. John H. Jones died on May 31, 1906. He and Almira are buried at the Temple Hill Cemetery, Geneseo, NY.

Thus ended the Abner-Sabra Jones branch of the Jacob-Hannah Jones family tree.

[1] https://en.wikipedia.org/wiki/Panic_of_1837.

[2] Oechsle, G. Russell and Boyce, Helen. *An Empire in Time: Clocks and Clock Makers of Upstate New York*, National Association of Watch & Clock Collectors, Inc., Columbia, PA, 2003.

[3] *Ontario County Mortgage Records:* Book 17, p. 466.

[4] *Ontario County Deed Records:* Book 70, pp. 59-60.

[5] *Ontario County Deed Records:* Book 70, pp. 454-455.

[6] Manke, Robert. *Genealogy of Abner Jones of Pittsfield*, (unpublished manuscript, revised October, 2020).

[7] *1850 U.S. Census for Avon, Livingston County, NY.*

[8] Manke, Robert. *Genealogy of Abner Jones of Pittsfield*, (unpublished manuscript, revised October, 2020).

[9] *Livingston County Deeds,* Book 50, p. 71.

[10] French's *Map of Ontario Co. New York.* Gillette's Publishing, Philadelphia, 1858. Library of Congress Map Collection.

[11] *1855 U.S. Census for Avon, Livingston Co., NY.*

[12] Rae & Otley. *Map of Livingston County, New York.* Smith & Gillette Publishers, Philadelphia, PA. 1852. Library of Congress Map Collection.

[13] *1860 U.S. Census for Avon, Livingston Co., NY*; research courtesy Robert Manke.

[14] *1870 U.S. Census for Avon, Livingston Co., NY.*

[15] *Livingston County Herald,* July 13, 1876, courtesy David Rosen; FindAGrave.com Abner Jones.

[16] *1865 U.S. Census for Livingston County, NY.*

[17] *Livingston County Deeds,* Book 100, p. 215.

[18] *U.S. Census Records for Livingston County, NY, 1850-1900*; research courtesy Robert Manke.

[19] *U.S. Census Records for Livingston County, NY, 1850; 1865; 1870, New York Civil War Muster Roll Abstracts 1861-1900*, Ancestry.com.

[20] Research courtesy Chris Bailey.

[21] *1850 and 1855 U.S. Census for Livingston County, NY.*

[22] *1870 U.S. Census Records for Livingston County, NY.*

IN CONCLUSION

Without Equal: The Clocks of Abner Jones of Bloomfield, New York

This enterprise began with the intention of clarifying, to the extent possible at this time and place, the history and extant examples of the work of clockmaker Abner Jones of Bloomfield, NY. Specifically, several basic questions were posed, including *"Where did he come from?" "When did he make his clocks?" "Where did he make his clocks?"* and *"What were his production totals?"* All research has its limits, but that reality notwithstanding, every effort has been made to develop each of these inquiries. An assessment of what we have learned can be outlined as follows.

Abner Jones, in all likelihood accompanied by his cousin Richard, arrived at the settlement of East Bloomfield, NY, from Pittsfield, NH, in 1818, where he established a brass foundry just off the village green while living in a nearby rented home. Abner and Richard soon were engaged in the making of tall clocks, as they had been trained in New Hampshire. The Jones tall clocks made at East Bloomfield are not labeled, but the movements are so distinctive, and so clearly derivative of those made by Abner's father Jacob at Pittsfield, NH, to be clearly identifiable. At least four Jones tall clocks have been identified by the author, and no doubt others exist. Three of those clocks feature distinctive cut-steel hands, which may provide a means to preliminarily identify the makers without having to examine the clock movement itself.

The Jones' tall clocks appear with dials obtained from both English and American sources. The interior of one tall clock case is inscribed in pencil with the date "1820" and the statement that the casemaker was "Daniel Miles." Miles was, indeed, a resident and, in fact, a neighbor of Abner and Richard Jones at the time, but while he can be identified as a store owner, his bona fides as a cabinet maker cannot be verified.

Living at Bloomfield throughout Abner Jones' clock production era was an exceptional cabinet maker named Simeon Deming. A member of a prominent cabinet making family from Wethersfield, CT, Simeon had worked at New York City and Stockbridge, MA, before moving to Bloomfield in 1813. This highly skilled individual remains a strong candidate as the maker of both tall and shelf clock cases for Abner Jones.

Evidence suggests that Abner and Richard relocated to a homestead in the town of Bloomfield just south of the village in 1824. Tall clock making at East Bloomfield ended by 1827, signaled, at least in part, by the parting of Richard and family from Bloomfield to Springwater, Livingston County, NY, by early 1828, where Richard was employed in "manufacturing and trades" and farming. Richard Jones died in 1846 at Springwater.

By 1831, Abner Jones had determined to resume clock making, joining a number of upstate New York makers in competition to produce distinctive, high-style, high-priced 8-day brass movement shelf clocks.

Some of Jones' early shelf clocks had dates and numbers stamped on their movements. Over time, very few clocks were dated, but clocks were intermittently numbered throughout the shelf clock production period.

Of the known Abner Jones shelf clocks with *time-and-strike* movements and inscribed movement numbers, the highest recorded number is 96, this giving rise to, and just possibly confirming, the notion that his total production may not have reached far beyond 100.

The shelf clock with the earliest known inscribed movement — dated 1831 — is the only one known with a timepiece (time-only) movement, and that clock movement is also stamped with the highest known inscribed movement number—150. This type of incongruity is common with respect to Abner Jones' shelf clock production. It is posited that he may have been intending to utilize separate number series for his time-and-strike and timepiece movements so started the latter at the higher number. The rarity of the timepiece likely indicates that few were made.

What appear to be the earliest shelf clock case styles fall into two groups. **Group One** models feature cornice tops, turned half columns, attractive and unique two-piece dials with gilt chapter rings and decorative spandrels (all with attractive, often folk-art designs), looking glasses (mirrors) in the doors and cabinet sections with drawers in the base. The **Group Two** cases reflect modest evolutions in the **Group One** design, including revised top moldings, new dials and hands, and more uniformity in case construction. A total of 17 **Group One and Two** surviving clocks have been documented. It appears likely that all of these clocks were produced at the town of East Bloomfield location.

In early 1835, Abner Jones and family moved a few miles west to the village and town of West Bloomfield, purchasing a 28-acre parcel fronting on the Ontario and

Genesee Turnpike (today's U.S. Route 20 and NY Route 5). The family lived in an existing house, and foundry and clock production took place in an adjacent manufacturing building. Updated case designs accompanied the move to West Bloomfield, documented by the helpful fact that several of the new models contained movements with stamped "1835" dates. Most of the cases produced in 1835 and on did not feature lower drawer sections.

For analysis purposes, the author has identified six post-1835 case styles, totaling 39 surviving clocks. Unlike the **Group One and Group Two** clocks, which appear to have been made in successive batches, the remainder of Abner Jones' shelf clock models appear to have been made and sold intermittently throughout the 1835-1840 period, perhaps by customer order.

The identified groupings include **Group Three – *Full Empire Cases;* Group Four – *Scroll Top Cases;* Group Five – *Sloped Cornice Top Cases Without Drawers;* Group Six – *Sharp Cornice Top Cases Without Drawers;* Group Seven – *Sharp Cornice Top Cases With Drawers;*** and **Group Eight – *Very Large Sharp Cornice Top Cases With Drawers***. Of the surviving shelf clocks, the most common case style, with 14 known examples, is that of **Group Four**, the cases with carved scroll splats and carved or turned columns without drawers in the base.

Among what are believed to be the post-1835 models, the surviving *time-and-strike* movement clock with the lowest numbered movement found to date is #48, and, as noted above, the highest is #96. Several late production clocks, including one seeming presentation model, drop the iconic Abner Jones two-piece dial arrangement.

This and other changes indicate that Jones' production and design efforts were continuing to evolve until the exigencies of the 1837 nationwide economic crisis and the revolutionary changes in American production and marketing methods brought his clock making enterprise to an end.

By 1840, Abner Jones was in apparent dire financial straits and in arrears in his mortgage payments to Charles Webb, from whom he had purchased his property at West Bloomfield in 1835. Webb brought suit in the New York courts, and on May 3, 1841, the Jones property, consisting of house, manufacturing building and farm land was sold at public auction on the steps of the Ontario County Courthouse at Canandaigua.

After leaving West Bloomfield, Abner, Sabra and family moved approximately 15 miles due west on the turnpike to the village of Avon, Livingston County. There they rented and the family later purchased a home on Prospect Street, and Abner resumed work as a brass founder. Sabra gave birth to the couple's fifth child, Alice, in 1842, but Sabra died soon thereafter due to complications. For the most part, Abner and his children continued to live together at the Prospect Street home into the 1870s.

Abner Jones died on July 12, 1876. Records show that his last days were spent in the Livingston County Alms [or Poor] House, suffering from dementia, a sad end for the man whose creativity remains so evident in his works.

Abner Jones' clock production in upstate New York can be seen as both a product of its time, in terms of its foundation in the artisanal (i.e., brass movement tall clock) tradition, and a bridge to the era of the mass production of clocks with interchangeable parts. If his work is presented as representative of the last gasp of the low-production, hand-built, tall case and shelf clock era, his examples should be distinctive and extraordinary, and they are.

In 2003, the author, with co-conspirator Helen Boyce, edited and produced the publication *"An Empire in Time: Clocks and Clock Makers of Upstate New York."* In that volume, over 150 individual clockmakers or merchandisers operating in upstate New York in the 18th, 19th, and 20th centuries were documented. Consider that crowded field and then add to that total the vastly greater numbers of other American makers operating in those years, especially those in Connecticut. In this light, the difficulty that confronted any individual maker in this era who was attempting to carve out a niche so distinctive, unusual and notable as to be found unique among his peers falls into focus.

Abner Jones, the maker of the clocks with the drawers, the clocks with the dials that open with the door, the clocks with handmade movements in the dawn of the age of mass production, the maker of shelf clocks of limited numbers but of unparalleled size and exuberant Empire style, achieved through his work a status that was evident from the first. The clocks, revered then as now, were and are simply without equal.

APPENDIX A

"Group One" Clock Characteristics

Flat (Cornice) Top; rounded or flat case sides; turned columns, 2 over 1 drawers (one exception), lower drawer with flat or rounded front; paw feet, dial with gilt chapter ring with small Arabic numerals (1 with Roman numerals) but 2 dials with larger gilt ring and Arabic numerals); steel hands with some replaced (?) brass hands; time-and-strike 8-day movement (1 timepiece only).

Clock ID#	Movement #	Date	Dial Type	Sec. Bit?	Hands	Drawers Lower Rd./Flat	Sides	Bell In Or Hole	Wall-paper?	Pulleys In/Out	EAE #	Provenance (Original Owner)
1-A	#150	1831	Gilt, Arabic	NA	Steel	3/1 Rd.	Round	NA	No	In	-	Fitch Family / Russ Oechsle
1-B	#96	-	Gilt, Arabic	Yes	Steel	2/1 Rd.	Flat	In	No	In	-	Wilder Family / Tom Grimshaw
1-C	#2	-	Gilt, Arabic	No	Steel	2/1 Rd.	Flat	In	No	Out	#40	Herb Nilson / Mark Chaplin
1-D	#3	-	Gilt, Arabic	Yes	Steel	2/1 Rd.	Round	In	Yes	In	#37	Larry Postle / Conrad Hummel
1-E	#6	1832	Gilt, Arabic	No	Steel	2/1 Flat	Round	In	Yes	Out	#23	Baker-White Family / National Watch & Clock Museum
1-F	-	-	Gilt, Arabic	Yes	Brass	2/1 Rd.	Round	In	Yes	Out	#13	Doug Blazey / George Goolsby / Ralph Pokluda
1-G	-	-	Gilt, Arabic	No	Brass	2/1 Flat	Flat	Hole	Yes	In	#14	? / Granger Homestead
1-H	-	-	Gilt, Roman*	Yes	Brass	2/1 Rd.	Round	Hole	No	In	#35	Dick Babel / Larry Postle
1-I	-	-	White, Arabic**	No	Brass	2/1 Rd.	Round	Hole	No	In	#27	Hoffman Museum
1-J	-	-	Gilt, Arabic	Yes	Brass	1 Rd.	Flat	Hole	No	In	-	J.R. Brundage / Clayton Smith / Skip Harlach / Russ Oechsle

*Numerals Replaced
**Restored

APPENDIX B
"Group Two" Clock Characteristics

Flat top over a 3" box; flat case sides; all clocks have the same turned columns; 2 over 1 drawers; lower drawer with flat or round front; paw feet; dial with large white chapter ring with Arabic numerals, no dials have seconds bits; all with 8-day time-and-strike movements, all with brass, heart-shaped hands, all with the same pattern of wallpaper inside the case.

Clock ID#	Movement #	Date	Dial Type	Sec. Bit?	Top Type	Hands	Drawers Round / Flat	Sides	EAE #	Provenance (Original Owner)
2-A	-	-	White, Arabic	No	Flat / Box	Brass	2/1 Flat	Flat	#31	Margaret Elle / E. Bloomfield H.S.
2-B	#4	-	White, Arabic	No	Flat / Box	Brass	2/1 Round	Flat	#26	Neal Henry / Don Lance / Russ Oechsle
2-C	-	-	White, Roman	No	Flat / Box	Brass	2/1 Flat	Flat	#21	Walter Southworth / Bob Kaltaler
2-D	-	-	White, Arabic	No	Flat / Box	Brass	2/1 Flat	Flat	#25	Pete Zaharis / Joe Galano / Steve Petrucelli
2-E	unk.	unk.	White, Arabic	No	Flat / Box	Brass	2/1 Flat	Flat	#30	Jim Van Wie / ?
2-F	-	-	White, Arabic	No	Flat / Box	Brass	2/1 Round	Flat	#10	Bryson Moore / National Watch & Clock Museum
2-G	-	-	White, Arabic	No	Flat / Box	Brass	2/1 Flat	Flat	-	? / John Fadden
2-H	-	-	White, Arabic	No	Flat / Box	?	Missing	Flat	-	Charles Parsons / ?

APPENDIX C

"Group Three" Clock Characteristics
Full Empire Cases

Cornice top Empire full half columns, double door, all with nonstandard small dials with Roman numerals; no dials with seconds bits; with or without feet, all with 8-day time-and-strike movements, brass hands.

Clock ID#	Movement #	Date	Dial Type	Sec. Bit?	Feet	Drawers	EAE #	Provenance (Original Owner)
3-A	-	1835	2Pc. Zinc	No	Yes	4	#8	*Steele Family*
3-B	-	-	1Pc. Zinc	No	No	None	#26	Auburn, NY Picker / Larry Postle / Russ Oechsle
3-C	unk.	-	Paint, Glass	No	No	None	-	Buel-Barr Study / ?

APPENDIX D

"Group Four" Clock Characteristics
Scroll Top Cases

Half columns either turned or carved with carved scrolls. No cabinet sections with drawers; no paw feet; none with original wallpaper; dials with Roman numerals; two dials are one piece; no dials with seconds bits; all with 8-day time-and-strike movements and brass hands.

Clock ID#	Movement #	Date	Dial Type	Top Type	Columns	Door Panel	EAE #	Provenance
4-A	-	1835	2 Piece	Carved Scroll	Turned	Wood	#17	? / Larry Postle
4-B	#49	-	2 Piece	Carved Scroll	Turned	Wood	-	Grover Greene / Lester Phillips / Anthony Braida
4-C	#59	-	2 Piece	Carved Scroll	Turned	Wood	#34	? / Joe Wyland
4-D	-	-	2 Piece	Carved Scroll	Turned	Wood	-	? / Ray Abernathy
4-E	-	-	2 Piece	Carved Scroll	Turned	Wood	-	Bob Albert / Tom Barrett
4-F	-	-	2 Piece	Carved Scroll	Carved	Wood	#43	Merritt's Antiques / Dave Rosen
4-G	-	-	1 Piece	Carved Scroll	Carved	Wood	-	? / Jim Dickinson / Dick Galluci / Dave & Dick Baker
4-H	-	-	2 Piece	Carved Scroll	Turned	Mirror	#20	Sheldon Hoch / ?
4-I	-	-	2 Piece	Carved Scroll	Carved	Mirror	-	Pete Zaharis / Dave Hadden / Larry Postle
4-J	#76	-	2 Piece	Carved Scroll	Carved	Mirror	#41	? / Jim Stehlik
4-K	#77	-	2 Piece	Carved Scroll	Carved	Mirror	#32	Mrs. Anton Long / Frank Boyce
4-L	-	-	2 Piece	Carved Scroll	Carved	Mirror	#5	Ed Haas / ?
4-M	-	-	2 Piece	Carved Scroll	Carved	Mirror	-	? / Russ Oechsle
4-N	-	-	1 Piece	Carved *Shell**	Turned	Rev. Paint*	#33	Jim Van Wie / ?

*Reliably reported as not original.

APPENDIX E

"Group Five" Clock Characteristics
"Sloped" Cornice Top Cases Without Drawers

"Sloped" cornice flat top, carved half columns, no drawers, no paw feet; dial with large, white chapter ring with Roman numerals, all with 8-day time-and-strike movements, brass hands. No clocks have dated movements.

Clock ID#	Movement #	Dial Numerals	Top Type	Columns	Door Panel	EAE #	Provenance (Original Owner)
LARGE CASE							
5-A	#48	Roman	Sloped Cornice	Carved	Mirror	#18	*Wheeler Family* / Pete Zaharis / Paul Hudson / EBHS
5-B	-	Roman	Sloped Cornice	Carved	Mirror	#3	Tom Grimshaw / Pete Zaharis / ?
MEDIUM CASE							
5-C	-	Roman	Sloped Cornice	Carved	Mirror	#2	Bob Ewald / Hoffman Clock Museum
SMALL CASE							
5-D	-	Roman	Sloped Cornice	Carved	Mirror	-	? / Joe Galano / Tom Poland
5-E	-	Roman	Sloped Cornice	Carved	Mirror	-	Doug Blazey / Photo from 1990 NAWCC National

APPENDIX F

"Group Six" Clock Characteristics
"Sharp" Cornice Top Cases Without Drawers

Sharp cornice flat top, carved or turned half columns, no drawers, no paw feet; dial with large, white chapter ring with Arabic or Roman numerals, all with 8-day time-and-strike movements, brass hands. No clocks have dated movements.

Clock ID#	Movement #	Dial Numerals	Top Type	Columns	Door Panel	EAE #	Provenance (Original Owner)
LARGE CASE							
6-A	#90 (bob)	Roman	Sharp Cornice	Carved	Mirror	#24	? / Ed Lafond
6-B	#91 (bob)	Roman	Sharp Cornice	Carved	Mirror	#38	George E. Barton / Tom Grimshaw / Chris Bailey / Ed Lafond
MEDIUM CASE							
6-C	#50	Roman	Sharp Cornice	Carved	Mirror	#36	Doug Evans / Jeff Baker
6-D	-	Roman	Sharp Cornice	Carved	Mirror	#9	*Steele Family* / Hamlin Family / Ontario Co. H.S.
6-E	#64	Arabic	Sharp Cornice	Carved	Mirror	#7	Doug Blazey / ?
6-F	#56	Roman	Sharp Cornice	Turned	Mirror	#19	Anthony Sposato / ?
6-G	-	Roman	Sharp Cornice	Turned	Wood	#42	Henry Sayward / ?
6-H	#87	Roman	Sharp Cornice	Turned	Mirror	#22	Hank Stegeman / Gary Lockwood
6-I	#95	Roman	Sharp Cornice	Carved	Mirror	#11	Seen at 1999 NAWCC Chicago National / ?

APPENDIX G

"Group Seven" Clock Characteristics
"Sharp" Cornice Top Cases With Drawers

Sloped and sharp cornice flat top cases, carved or turned columns, with 1-4 drawers in cabinet base, paw feet; dial with large, white chapter ring, all with Roman numerals, all with 8-day time-and-strike movements, brass hands.

Clock ID#	Movement #	Top Type	Columns	# Drawers	Door Panel	EAE #	Provenance (Original Owner)
7-A	#57	Sharp Cornice	Carved	3	Mirror	#16	*Parmele Family* / Joe Wyland
7-B	#65	Sharp Cornice	Carved	1	Mirror	#12	Doug Blazey / Jim Blazey / Dave Ewbanks
7-C	-	Sharp Cornice	Turned	3	Mirror	#1	? / Evan Edwards / ?
7-D	-	Sharp Cornice	Turned	1	Mirror	#6	Doug Blazey / Pete Zaharis / ?

APPENDIX H

"Group Eight" Clock Characteristics
Very Large "Sharp" Cornice Top Cases With Drawers

Sharp cornice flat top cases, turned half columns, with 4 drawers in cabinet base, all with turned feet; two-piece dials, all with Roman numerals, all with 8-day time-and-strike movements, brass hands. No clocks are dated.

Clock ID#	Movement #	Top Type	Columns	# Drawers	Door Panel	EAE #	Provenance (Original Owner)
8-A	-	Sharp Cornice	Turned	4	Mirror	-	Alfred Burnham / John Davis / Steve Petrucelli / Russ Oechsle
8-B	-	Sharp Cornice	Flat Turned	4	Mirror	#15	*Morse Family* / Mabel Converse / Ruth Pierce / Kathy Bowerman
8-C	#88	Sharp Cornice	Flat Turned	4	Mirror	#4	Hank Stegeman / Pete Zaharis / ?

APPENDIX I

Evan Edwards' Inventory of Abner Jones Clocks

This list, consisting of the EAE numbers and the names shown below in BOLD type, was provided to the author in 2003 by Evan Edwards, along with his photograph file, which the author was allowed to copy. All of the additional information noted below for each clock was compiled by the author, who is responsible for any questions as to accuracy. Photos do not exist for several listings (EAE #29 and #39), and neither of these clocks has been located by the author. In addition, at least one owner notation (EAE #28) and the associated clock remain unidentified.

EAE #	Edwards Recorded Owner (Comments Added by the Author)
1	**Evan Edwards** bought at Lebanon, NH, – *Later 3-dwr, Turned Columns, Late Sharp Top Cornice*
2	**Theurer** (?) Bob Ewald, Rochester, NY, to Hoffman Museum – *Late Short Carved Col. & Sloped Top Cornice*
3	**Hank Stegeman** to Tom Grimshaw to Pete Zaharis to ? – *Late Large Carved Col. & Sloped Top Cornice, no drawers, like #18 but not the same clock!*
4	**Hank Stegeman** to Pete Zaharis to ? – *Tall Late Sharp Top Cornice Very Tall with 4 dwrs. #88 on movement*
5	**Ed Haas** to ? – *Scroll Top Carved Column*
6	**Doug Blazey** to Pete Zaharis to ? – *Sharp Top Cornice & Column with 3 drawers, no box, wallpaper, turned columns, w/o paint or stenciling, flat sides, round lower drawer, offset brass straps attach movement to spacer brackets, later dial later hands.*
7	**Doug Blazey** to ? – *Clock #64. Short case Sharp Top cornice & carved columns Arabic numerals on dial*
8	**Steele Family** – *Clock stamped 1835, Empire Sharp Top Cornice w/box, maple columns, 4 dwrs, smaller dial/door, lacks feet, G.W. Berry stamped on movement*
9	**Lena Steele** to David Hamlin to Ontario County Historical Society – *Short case Late Sharp Top Cornice with carved columns, no drawers*
10	**Bryson Moore** to the National Watch & Clock Museum – *donated after his passing by his wife. Group Two flat top cornice w/ box, 3 dwr. lacks feet*
11	**Chicago National** to ? – *#95 Sharp Top cornice & carved col.; inner dial painted gold, seconds bit, also #16 on lower front of back plate. Same style case as EAE #9*
12	**Doug Blazey** to Jim Blazey to Dave Ewbank – *Late "Tall" Sharp Top Cornice and Carved Column Case with one drawer and paw feet. Has number #65*
13	**Mrs. Munson**; Doug Blazey to George Goolsby to Ralph Pokluda – *Group One Early Dial, Flat Top no box, turned columns, 3 dwr., Early hands*
14	**Granger Homestead**, Canandaigua – *Group One, Early Dial, heart hands, Flat top, no box, 3 dwr. Turned columns.*
15	**Mrs. Converse, daughter Mrs. Pierce** at Clifton Springs to Kathy Bowerman – *Flat Top Tall (See #4 above) with 4 dwrs.*
16	**Harmon Parmele**, East Bloomfield to Joseph Wyland – *Late Sharp top cornice, 3 dwr., seconds bit. Has movement number #57, plus mark below TS great wheel of #7.*
17	**Larry Postle** – *Scroll Top and Turned column, panel in door, R.T. Reynolds 1835 stamped on back plate. Never had a center dial.*
18	**Pete Zaharis** to Paul Hudson to (Donation) East Bloomfield Historical Society – *Sloped Top Cornice Tall (late) carved columns, #48 on movement, Edwards notes epicyclical maintaining power, case like #24, Similar to #38*
19	**Tony Sposato** to? – *#56 on movement, short Sharp Top cornice & turned and stenciled columns, same as EAE #22. Sold at Bourne Auction in 1986; current owner unknown.*
20	**Sheldon Hoch** to ? – *Scroll Top and Turned column, Center dial replaced?*
21	**Bob Kaltaler** – *Group Two, Flat top with Box, 3 dwr. Turned columns. Flat dwr. Fronts*

Continued on page 174.

APPENDIX I (Continued)

EAE #	Edwards Recorded Owner (Comments Added by the Author)
22	**Hank Stegeman** to Gary Lockwood – *Sharp Top Short case, turned columns in case the size of the carved column and splat cases. Stenciled columns, #87 on movement; originally from Lockport, NY*
23	**Mrs. Van Halla**; Baker-White Family to NAWCC (Assisted by NAWCC Chapter 13) – *Group One: Early dial, early hands, #6 and 1832 on movement (also #3 on left side of movement), Flat top, no box, round sides, turned columns, wallpaper in case*
24	**Ed LaFond** – *Sharp Top Cornice Tall, Late with carved columns, #90 on pendulum bob, planetary winding per Evan*
25	**Pete Zaharis** to ? to Steve Petrucelli – *Group Two Flat top with box, 3 dwrs, turned columns, wallpaper in case*
26	**Don Lance** to Russ Oechsle – *Group Two Flat top with box, turned and stenciled columns, 3 dwrs, #4 Wallpaper in case.*
27	**Hoffman Clock Museum** – *Group One Flat top no box but with later standard dial and hands, 3 dwr., carved columns*
28	**Gahm** *(No idea what this meant, but research found a collector from Auburn, NY, named Ralph Gehm whose collection was apparently sold in 2002. Search is ongoing. Edwards had no extant photos).*
29	**Doug Blazey** to ? *(No extant photos)*
30	**Jim Van Wie** to ? – *Group Two, Flat Top with box, turned columns, 3 dwr.*
31	**Margaret Elle** to East Bloomfield Historical Society – *Group Two Flat top with box, turned columns, 3 dwr., repainted good dial, wallpaper in case.*
32	**Mrs. Anton Long** to Frank Boyce in 1995 – *Scroll top case Carved column and, #77. Scroll replaced*
33	**Jim Van Wie** to ? – *Shell-carved splat & carved column with full dial (repainted incorrectly with Weare, NH, reference. Top replaced.)*
34	**Hodges** (?) to ? to Joseph Wyland – *Scroll Top with turned columns and solid panel door. Movement #56.*
35	**Richard Babel** to Larry Postle – *Group One, Early Dial w/ seconds bit and Roman numerals, likely repainted, later hands, may be replacements, Flat top, no box, turned columns, 3 dwr. Lacking feet*
36	**Doug Evans** to Jeff Baker – *Short Sharp Top Cornice and carved column case, #50 on movement*
37	**Mrs. Munson** to Larry Postle to Conrad Hummel – *Group One, Early Dial, Early hands, Flat no Box, turned columns, seconds bit, 3 dwr., #3 on movement, wallpaper*
38	**Geo. E. Barton**, Clifton Springs, NY, to Tom Poland, NY, to Ed & Virginia Lafond, PA – *Large Sharp Top Cornice case with carved columns, #91 on pendulum bob.*
39	**Vinnie Versage** *(No extant photo)*
40	**Herb Nilson**, VT to Mark Chaplin – *Group One, Early dial, early hands (now replaced with later brass heart hands), Flat top no box, round sides, movement #2 on front of back plate, 40" 3-drawer.*
41	**Paul Walker** to Jim Stehlik – *Scroll top case with carved columns. #76 on Movement*
42	**Henry Sayward** to ? – *Short Sharp Top Cornice & turned Columns, oval glass in lower door wood panel*
43	**Dave Rosen** – *Scroll top and carved columns, wood panel door. (Note: Evan Edwards had assigned this number to the clock that was already #14. He had assigned this clock #40 but had already assigned that number to the clock noted above, so I have assigned this clock #43!)*

APPENDIX J

Abner Jones Shelf Clocks by the Numbers

A listing of the known Abner Jones shelf clocks exhibiting numbers and/or dates inscribed on the clocks, generally on the movements but in several instances on the pendulum bobs.

# and / or Date	Group #	Clock # & Notes
"1831" and "150"	Group One	Timepiece Clock 1-A.
"2"	Group One	Clock 1-C.
"3"	Group One	Clock 1-D.
"4"	Group Two	Clock 2-B.
"6" and "1832"	Group One	Clock 1-E.
"1835" "G. W. Berry"	Group Three	Clock 3-A, Full Col. & Cornice; 4 dwrs.
"1835" "R. T. Reynolds"	Group Four	Clock 4-A, Scroll Top carved cols. No inner dial.
"48"	Group Five	Clock 5-A, Large Sloped cornice carved col.
"49"	Group Four	Clock 4-B, Scroll Top Carved cols., mirror door.
"50"	Group Six	Clock 6-C, Medium Sharp cornice carved col.
"56"	Group Six	Clock 6-F, Medium Sharp cornice & turned col.
"57"	Group Seven	Clock 7-B, Late Large sharp cornice and carved col. with drawers.
"59"	Group Four	Clock 4-B, Scroll Top Turned col. wood door.
"64"	Group Six	Clock 6-E, Medium Sharp cornice & carved col.
"65"	Group Six	Clock 6-G, Medium Sharp cornice & carved col.
"71"	-	Movement from Unknown Clock - Edwards Photo.
"76"	Group Four	Clock 4-I, Scroll Top carved col. w/ mirror.
"77"	Group Four	Clock 4-J, Scroll Top carved col. w/ mirror.
"87"	Group Six	Clock 6-H, Medium Sharp cornice & turned col. w/ mirror.
"88"	Group Eight	Clock 8-C, Extra Large Sharp cornice & turned col. w/ 4-dwr. cabinet base.
"90"	Group Six	Clock 6-A, Large Cornice & carved col. # on Pend. Bob
"91"	Group Six	Clock 6-B, Large Cornice & carved col. # on Pend. Bob
"95"	Group Six	Clock 6-H, Medium Sharp Cornice & carved col. Also "16" on back plate
"96"	Group One	Clock 1-B, Also has "17" on back plate

NOTE: *As of the time of publication, 23 clocks and one loose movement had been identified with inscribed numbers or notations.*

RESEARCH ILLUSTRATIONS

Illustrations completed by the author during the development of this publication.

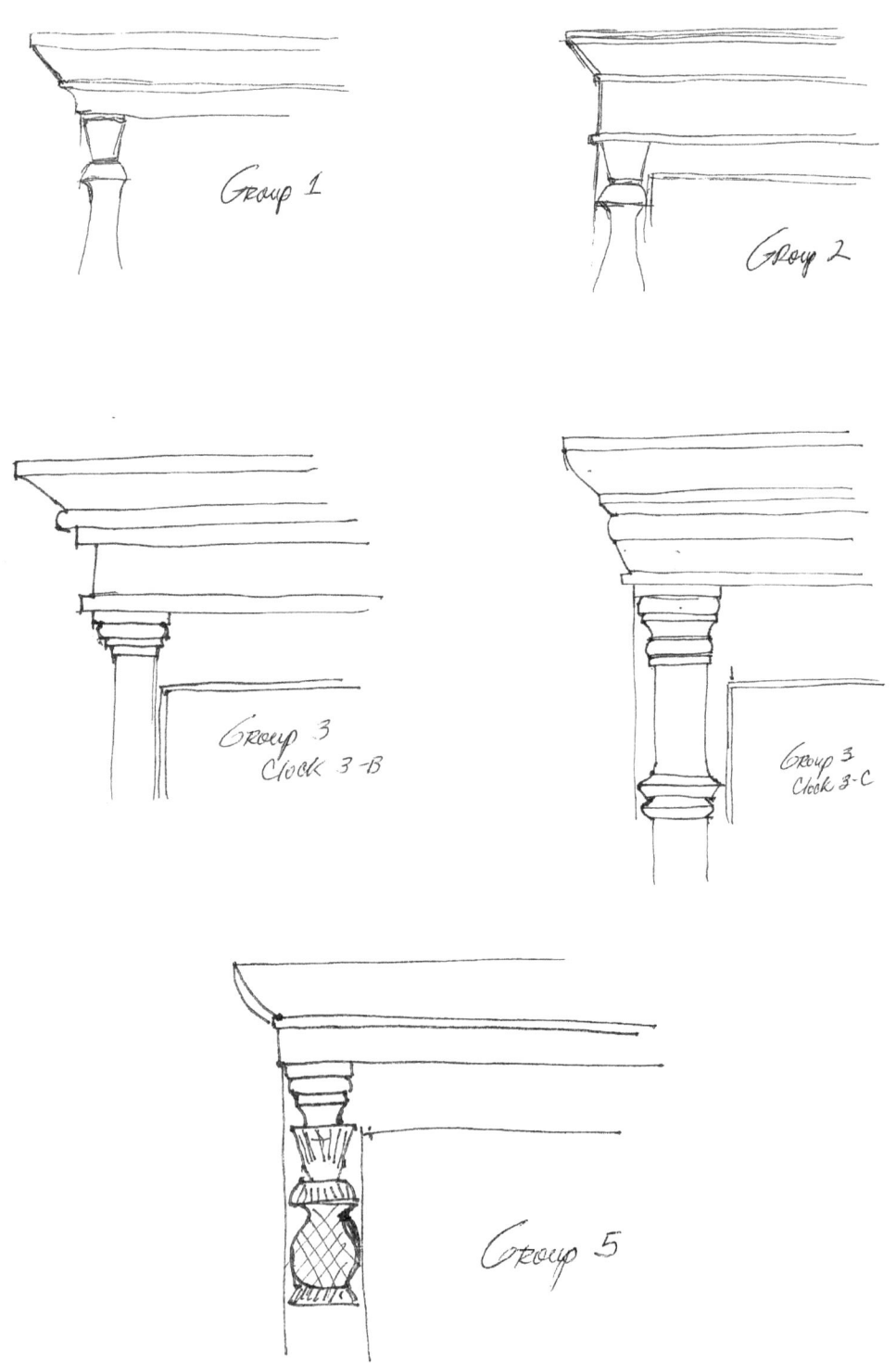

176 • Research Illustrations

ACKNOWLEDGEMENTS

Without the assistance of the following individuals and institutions, this work would not have been possible. Their names are noted below. The author apologizes to any contributor that I may have missed!

Robert Manke
Chris Bailey
Frederick Chris Tahk (dec.)
Pat Hagans
Larry Postle
Sam & Matt Cottone; Cottone's Auctions
Mark Chaplin
Jeff Steele
Hank Stegeman
Dave Richardson
Larry Berkson, Pittsfield, NH, Historian
Patti Philippon, ACWM
George Goolsby
Conrad Hummel
Judi Stuart, E. Bloomfield, NY, Historian
Terry Brotherton
Jeff Baker
Gary Lockwood
Dave Hadden
Jim Stehlik
Chuck Roeser
Jim Blazey
Kathy Bowerman
Paul Hudson
Eric Hooker, Hoffman Clock Museum
Marci Diehl, Ontario Co. Historical Society
NAWCC Museum Collection
Steve Petrucelli
Paul Friday, New Hampshire Hist. Soc.
Charles Parsons (dec.)
Robert Cheney

Mary Jane Dapkus
Tom Grimshaw
Frank & Helen Boyce
Bob Kaltaler
Wilma Townsend, OCHS
Marilyn & Ross Fitch
Joe Wyland
Joel Steele
Virginia & Will Lafond
Dick Baker
Pat Tally, W. Bloomfield, NY, Historian
Tom Manning
Ralph Pokluda
Ken McHenry
Lindy Larson
Ben Orszulak
Tom Poland
John Fadden
Tom Barrett
Anthony Briada
Steve Sanborn
Bud Breed
Ray Abernathy
Lowell Ling
East Bloomfield Historical Society
Martha Herbik, Granger Homestead
American Watch & Clock Museum
Dave Ewbank
Ward Francillon (dec.)
The Delaneys – Delaneys Antique Clocks
Laura Taylor, NAWCC

INDEX

A

Abernathy, Ray 168, 176
Adams,
    Abner 11, 12, 13, 24
    Elmer W. 70, 71, 147, 148, 160
    Jonathan 24
    John 11
    Myron 12, 13
Albany, NY 8
Amber, NY 67, 160
American Clock & Watch Museum 62, 150, 176
Antrim, NH 41
Appomattox, VA 93
Arnold, Jared, Jr. 67, 71, 160
Auburn, NY 27, 28, 41, 67, 70, 160
Auburn State Prison 69
Aurelius, MI 73
Avery, Austin 11, 12
Avon, NY 160-162, 164

B

Babel, Dick 165, 174
Bailey, Chris .... Preface, 3, 6, 14, 23, 148, 156, 162, 170, 176
Baker,
    Blaze 43
    Family 43
    Jasper Gideon 43
    Jeff 140, 170, 174, 176
    Ortes 43
    Persus Hughes 43
    Dave 168
    Dick 168, 176
Baker-White Family 43, 54, 165, 174
Balch, David 2
Barr, Lockwood 154
Barrett, Tom 166, 176
Barton, George E. 170, 174
Batavia, NY 52

Beers, D. G.,
    Map of Ontario County, NY 12, 23, 54, 65, 77, 93, 111
Bemis, James D. 8
Berkson, Larry 2, 4, 176
Berry, Alvina 73
Berry, Gilman Ward 73, 76, 77, 149, 173, 175
Berry, Roxie 73
Berry, Ward 73
Birge, John 67
Blazey,
    Doug 45, 98, 107, 115, 117, 165, 169, 170, 171, 173, 174
    Jim 173, 176
Bloomfield Academy 9, 10
Bloomfield Meeting House 8
Bloomfield, Town of 7
Bloomfield, Town of East 7-14, 18, 53, 54, 58, 60, 64, 65, 71-73, 77, 89, 91, 93, 106, 107, 113, 123, 163, 164
Bloomfield, Town of West ... 7, 9, 11, 43, 54, 64, 65, 66, 70, 71, 76, 112, 146, 160, 163,164
Bloomfield, Village of East 8-14, 16, 22-25, 93, 106, 107, 160-163
Bourne, Richard A. & Co. 108, 111
Bowen, Peter 11
Bowerman, Kathy 123, 124, 172, 173, 176
Boyce, Frank & Helen .... Preface, 83, 168, 174, 176
Bradford, MA 2
Breed, Bud 176
Briada, Anthony 79, 168, 176
Bristol, CT 67, 154
Bristol, NY 33, 37
Bronson,
    Flavius J. 24, 25
    Sally 24
Brotherton, Terry 87, 176
Brundage, J.R. 165
Buel-Barr Study 154-159, 167
Buel, Carlton 154

Buel, Daniel W. 11, 12, 18
Buffalo, NY 8, 148
Burnham, Alfred 123, 172
Burt, Edward 156

C

Canandaigua, NY 8, 14, 123, 160, 164
Cayuga County, NY 27
Cayuga Lake 70
Chaplin, Mark 165, 174, 176
Cheney, Robert 91, 176
Chillicothe, OH 71, 148
Clifton Springs, NY 173, 174
Cone, A. 25
Conesus, NY 22
Converse,
    Louis H. 123
    Ruth 123
    Mabel 172, 173
Cottone's Auctions, Inc. 19, 20, 46, 61, 67, 68, 70, 80, 82, 97, 102, 116, 117, 120, 121, 125, 176
Covert, Peter 93
Curtis, Joel 22

D

Dapkus, Mary Jane .... Preface, 176
Davis, John 172
Delaney Antiques, Inc. 147, 176
Deming & Mills 89
Deming,
    Adelia 91
    James 89
    Judson Keith 91
    William 91
    Simeon 18, 89, 90, 91, 163
Dials, One-Piece 84
Dickinson, Jim 168
Diehl, Marci 176
Dow, Hanna 2

E

East Bloomfield .... (See Bloomfield)

East Bloomfield Congregational Church 8-11
East Bloomfield Historical Society 9, 58, 91, 93, 94, 111, 166, 169, 173, 174, 176
East Bloomfield Green 9, 10, 18, 163
East Bloomfield
    Lot #62 24-26
    Lot #77 .... 24, 25
East Haddam, CT 147, 149
Edwards, Evan .... Preface, 3, 6, 11, 23, 43, 45, 50, 52, 54, 60, 62, 72, 73, 74, 77, 81, 88, 106, 108, 109, 110, 111, 115, 118, 119, 123, 124, 128, 130, 137, 139, 143, 171, 173
Elle, Margaret 58, 166, 174
Epicyclic Maintaining Power 50, 101
Erie Canal 22, 26, 70
Evans, Doug 170, 174
Ewald, Bob 169, 173
Ewbank, Dave 173, 176

F

Fadden, John 63, 111, 166, 176
Farmer's Store, East Bloomfield 18
Fitch,
    Family 165
    Horace 33
    Horace W. 33
    Joshua 33
    Marilyn 176
    Ross Andrew 33, 176
    Walter Miller 33
    Walter R. 33
Francillon, Ward .... Preface, 147, 156, 176
French, J.H. 7, 23, 54, 162
Friday, Paul 176

G

Gallucci, Dick 168, 176
Gahm 174
Galano, Joe 166, 169
Gauss Rd., Bloomfield, NY 91
Gehm, Ralph 174
Geneseo, NY 19, 22, 162
Gillette, John E. 12

Golden Gavel Antiques, LLC 17
Graham, Adaline 162
 Patrick 162
Granger Homestead 48, 50, 165, 173, 176
Grant, U.S. 93
Green,
 Grover 168
 Jeannette 43
 Marion Baker 43
Griffith Family 43
Grigg, David & Daniel 148
Grimshaw, Tom .... Preface, 16, 38, 39, 40, 54, 129, 138, 148, 165, 169, 170, 173, 176
Goolsby, George 165, 173, 176
Group One – Group Eight Clocks .... (See Abner Jones Clocks)

H

Haas, Ed 168, 173
Hadden, Dave 168, 176
Hagans, Pat .... Preface, 174, 176
Hall,
 James H. 65, 160
 John T. 161
 William 161
Ham, Robert 14
Hamlin,
 David 173
 Elisha 24
 Family 170
 Philo 24
Harlach, Skip 165
Herbik, Martha 176
Herkimer, NY 26
Herkimer County, NY 26
Hickox,
 Burton 161
 Lucy .... (See Jones, Lucy)
 Sabra .... (See Jones, Sabra)
 William 11
Hilton, NY 37
History of Pittsfield, NY 2
Hoadley, Silas 22
Hobart, Harvey 10

Hoch, Sheldon 168, 173
Hodges 174
Hoffman Clock Museum 50, 51, 52, 95, 96, 165, 169, 173, 174, 176
Hooker, Eric 176
Hotchkiss & Benedict 41, 69, 71, 160
Hudson, Paul 93, 169, 173, 176
Hummel, Conrad 165, 176

I

Ingham County, MI 73
Ingraham,
 E. & Co. 154
 Edward 154, 156
 Elias 67
 Dudley 154, 156
Ithaca, NY 93, 123
Ives,
 C. & L. C. 67
 Joseph 54, 67, 77

J

Jackson, Andrew 160
Jerome, Chauncey 148
Johns, Andrew 24
Jones, Abner – Weare, NH 3, 4, 6, 84, 88
Jones, Abner at Avon, NY 160, 161, 162, 164
 at East Bloomfield Village of 8-24
 at East Bloomfield Town of 24-63
 at Pittsfield, NH 2, 3, 4, 6, 8
 at West Bloomfield Town of 64-66
Jones, Abner – Clocks
 Shelf Clocks – Case Styles
 Group One 27-53, 55-60, 71, 74, 112, 117, 127, 129, 140, 141, 144, 154, 163-165, 173-175
 Group Two 41, 50, 53, 55-60, 71, 112, 117, 127, 140, 163, 164, 173-175
 Group Three 71, 72, 76, 127, 149, 156, 164, 167
 Group Four 74-84, 92, 127, 141, 164, 168, 175
 Group Five 92-100, 101, 127, 141, 150, 164, 169, 175
 Group Six 92, 100-111, 127, 141, 146, 164, 170, 175
 Group Seven 92, 112-120, 127, 164, 171, 175

Group Eight 120-125, 127, 150, 154, 156, 164, 172, 175
Sharp Cornice Top Cases 92, 101-111, 118, 164
Sloped Cornice Top Cases 92-100, 164
Tall Clocks................. 14-22, 26, 27, 31, 35, 53, 73, 89, 163, 164
Timepiece.................................. 27-35, 53, 72, 126, 130, 131, 137, 138, 146, 163, 165, 175

Shelf Clocks – Characteristics
Back Plate Cutouts.............................. 127-129, 134
Brass Mounting Strips....................... 131-139
Door Latches 105, 115, 123, 139, 140, 141
Door Pulls 143
Drawer Pulls 142
Hands 143, 144
Pendulum Bobs 143, 145
Keys 139
Plate Pillar Posts 137-139
Weights 139

Shelf Clocks by Number & Date 146, 175
Jones,
Alice A... 160, 162, 164
Almira 24, 160, 162
Andrew.. 24
Bildad 2
Carlos 22
Charles 24, 160, 161
Hannah 2, 3
Huldah 2
Jacob 2, 3, 4, 8, 14, 15, 22
Tall Clocks.. 2, 4, 5
James... 2, 3, 4, 8
John 2, 3, 4, 8
John H.. 22
Jonathan 2, 3, 4, 162
Joseph 2, 3, 4, 8, 22
Lucinda 22
Lucy (Hickcox)................................. 11, 12, 22, 162
Mary 2
Miriam.. 2
Nathan 2
Oliver C. 24, 160, 161
Richard 3, 4, 8, 11, 12, 14, 20, 22, 24, 162, 163
Sabra (Hickcox).................... 11, 12, 24, 25, 60, 64, 160, 161, 164
Sarah 161
William 20
William W. 24, 160
Joslin, Hampton 24

K

Kaltaler, Bob.. 166, 173, 176
Kellogg, Thomas... 24
Kinsman, Jennie 93
Knowlton Corners, NH 2

L

Lafond,
Ed... 170, 174
Virginia.. 174, 176
Will 176
Lance, Don 166, 174
Lansing, MI 73
Larson, Lindy 176
Lebanon, NH... 115
Lee, Robert E. 93
Lima, NY 162
Ling, Lowell 176
Livingston County, NY 18, 22, 23, 24, 89, 160-163
Livingston County Alms House 161, 164
Livingston County Map... 161
Lockwood, Gary....................................... 170, 173, 176
Long, Mrs. Anton 168, 174

M

Mandeville, Henry.. 10
Manning, Tom.. Preface, 176
Manke, Robert.. Preface, 3, 4, 6, 8, 23, 54, 77, 162, 176
Mansfield,
Don 111
Family 172
Marcellus, NY.. 67, 69, 160
Markham, Chauncey 10
Marshall & Adams.. 70, 71
Marshall, Chauncey 70, 71
Mason, MI 73
McHenry, Ken 20, 176
McHume, Catherine 161
Mendon, NY 7
Merrills, Franklin M. 147, 148

Miles, Daniel 10, 12, 18, 89, 163
Mills & Deming 89, 90
Mills, William 89, 90
Mitchell, Isaac 18, 89
Moore, Bryson 166, 173
Morse,
    Edward H. 123
    Ida 123
    John 123
    Mabel 123
Munger,
    Asa 26, 27, 28, 30, 41, 67, 69
    Asa & Co. 69
Munson,
    Mrs. 173, 174
    R.C. 9, 10

N

National Association of Watch & Clock
Collectors (NAWCC) .... Preface, 43
    Chapter #13 .... 43, 174
    Museum, Columbia, PA 166, 174, 176
    National Convention, Chicago, 1992 ... 110, 170, 173
    National Convention, Houston, 1999 ...... 98, 99, 108,
    111, 169
National Gallery of Art 89
New York Route 5 .... 8, 65, 164
Newark, NY 50, 95
Newburyport, MA 2
New York City, NY 89, 90, 163
Nilson, Herb 41, 165, 174
Nine Mile Creek, Marcellus, NY 67

O

Oechsle, Russ .. Preface, 23, 54, 77, 162, 165, 166, 167, 168, 172, 174
Oechsle, G.R. & Boyce, Helen
    An Empire In Time .... Preface, 23, 54, 77, 148, 162, 164
Old Clock Club of Boston 156
Onondaga County, NY 67
Ontario County, NY 7, 8, 11, 12, 14, 23, 25, 33, 54, 60, 64, 77, 91, 93, 106, 107, 111, 160, 161, 162, 164

Ontario County Courthouse 160, 164
Ontario County Map 7, 12, 13, 25, 64, 65, 160, 161
Ontario County Historical Society 14-17, 23, 106, 170, 173, 176
Ontario & Genesee Turnpike 8, 164
Ontario Repository 8, 9
Orszulak, Ben 176
Owen, Edward 14, 15, 17

P

Palmer, Brooks .... Preface
Parsons, Charles 6, 148, 166, 176
Page Auctioneers & Appraisers 52, 53
Page,
    Emma 10
    Leonard 9, 10
    Sarah 10
    Stephan 9, 10, 12
Page & Jones 8, 9
Parks, Christopher 24
Panic of 1837 70
Parmele,
    Alonson 60, 64
    Family 113, 171
    G.N. 24, 25, 60
    Harmon 173
Parrish,
    Cora 43
    Griffith 43
    Louise 43
Partridge, Albert 156
Patterson, Thomas 160
Petrucelli, Steve 166, 172, 174, 176
Petersburg, VA 73
Phelps & Gorham's Purchase 11
Phillips, Lester 168
Philippon, Patti .... Preface, 176
Pierce,
    Caroline 123
    Robert 123
    Ruth 172, 173
Piffard, NY 22

Pilsbury,
  David 160
  William 160
Pittsfield, NH 2-6, 8, 14, 20, 23, 54, 73, 163
Planetary Winding.....(See Epicyclic Maintaining Power)
Plymouth Hollow,CT.. 93
Porter, Josiah 10
Postle, Larry 165, 167, 168, 173, 174, 176
Pokluda, Ralph.............................. 129, 165, 173, 176
Poland, Tom 169, 174, 176
Prindle, William 18, 89

Q

Quaker Meeting House, Pittsfield, NH....................... 2

R

Rae & Otley 161, 162
Reynolds, R.T. 76, 173
Richardson, Dave 176
Rochester, NY.. 109, 123
Roeser, Chuck 176
Rosen, Dave... 162, 168, 174
Royalton, NY 162
Royce, Harold.. 93

S

Sack, Israel 89
Sanborn, Steve 176
Sayward, Henry...................................... 109, 170, 174
Seabrook, NH... 2
Second Bank of the United States 160
Seneca & Cayuga Canal... 70
Seneca Falls, NY 70, 160
Seneca Lake, NY 70
Seth Thomas Clock Co. 93
Smith, Clayton 52, 165
  Phillip.. 67-71, 160
  R. Pearsall.. 23, 54
Southworth, Walter 166
Springwater, NY 22, 23, 24, 163

Sposato, Anthony 108, 170, 173
Steele,
  Family 72, 73, 74, 167, 170, 173
  Jeff.. 74, 150, 176
  Joel 176
Steele (*continued*),
  Joseph Stanley 74
  Lena 173
  Oran 74
  Stanley Oran 74
  William 24
Stegeman, Henry (Hank) ... 109, 123, 170, 172, 173, 176
Stewart, Judi... 8, 176
Stockbridge, MA... 91, 163

T

Tahk, Frederick (Chris) 114, 126, 134-138, 148, 176
Tally, Pat... 54, 176
Taylor, Snowden...................................... 23, 33, 54, 77
Temple Hill Cemetery.. 22
Terry, Eli 20, 22, 26, 54
Thomas,
  Seth 22
  Clock Co. 93
Theurer 173
Timby Solar Clock... Preface
Totman, Asahel C. 93, 106, 111
Townsend, Wilma.. 176

U

U.S. Route 20 .... 8, 65, 160, 164

V

Van Halla, Mrs. 174
Van Wie, Jim 166, 168, 174
Versage, Vinnie 174
Victor, NY...................................... 7, 98, 106, 115, 117

W

Walker, Paul 174
Washington, George 89

Webb, Charles 64, 160
Webster, Julia Wilder 37
West Bloomfield .... (See Bloomfield)
West, Nathan 24
Wethersfield, CT 89, 163
Wheeler,
    Benjamin 14
    D.C. 93
    Family 14, 169
    John 14
    George 14
    Remember 14
    Twiney 14
Whitaker, John 93
White, Hazel Parrish 43
Whiting, Riley, Jr. 22
Wilder,
    Erastus 37
    Family 37, 165
    Joseph 37
    Julia 37
Willson, Harold 123
Wilson,
    Jonah 24
    Nathan 24
Wolcott, Oliver 89
Wright, Elisha 24
Wycoff, Clara & Esther 93
Wyland, Joe 168, 171, 173, 174, 176

X, Y, Z

Yale University Library 90, 91
York, NY 18, 22, 89
Young, E. Harold 2
Young, Mary 161
Zaharis, Pete 93, 123, 166, 168, 169, 171-174

About the Author

G. Russell Oechsle is a long-time researcher of upstate New York clocks and clockmakers. He is the co-author of *An Empire in Time: Clocks and Clock Makers of Upstate New York* and author of *Good for a Time*. He is a Fellow of the American Clock & Watch Museum and a Star Fellow of the National Association of Watch & Clock Collectors.

Front Cover Photo Credits:
Left: Cottone's Auctions;
Center: Oechsle;
Right: Cottone's Auctions

Back Cover Photo Credits:
Clockwise from upper left:
Oechsle;
Tom Grimshaw;
Ken McHenry;
Oechsle

ISBN 979-8-9859967-0-8

Join thousands of other watch and clock enthusiasts by becoming a member today!
Visit nawcc.org/join/ to learn more.

www.ingramcontent.com/pod-product-compliance
Lightning Source LLC
Chambersburg PA
CBHW061211230426
43665CB00032B/2981